Sonia M. Baccari de Godoy
Cris Gontow
Marcello Marcelino

English Pronunciation for Brazilians

/ˈɪŋglɪʃ prəˌnʌnsɪˈeɪʃən fər brəˈzɪlɪənz/

The Sounds of American English

14ª Reimpressão

How to listen to the audio p. 288

Assistente editorial
Gabriela Canato

Capa e projeto gráfico
Paula Astiz

Editoração eletrônica
Priscila Arícia Neto / Paula Astiz Design

Ilustrações
Rafael Dourado

Áudio – Locutores
Cory Willis
Melody Grissom
Renata Steuer
Marcello Marcelino

Dados Internacionais de Catalogação na Publicação (CIP)
(Câmara Brasileira do Livro, SP, Brasil)

Godoy, Sonia
English pronunciation for brazilians : the sounds of american English : Sonia Godoy, Cris Gontow, Marcello Marcelino. – São Paulo : Disal, 2006.

ISBN 978-85-89533-70-6

1. Inglês – Estudo e ensino – Brasileiros 2. Inglês – Pronúncia por estrangeiros 3. Inglês – Uso I. Gontow, Cris. II. Marcelino, Marcello. III. Título.

06-5796 CDD-428

Índices para catálogo sistemático:

1. Pronúncia : Inglês para brasileiros : Lingüística aplicada 428
2. Inglês para brasileiros : Lingüística aplicada : Pronúncia 428

Al. Mamoré, 911, sala 107, Alphaville
06454-040, Barueri, SP
Tel./Fax: (11) 4195-2811

Visite nosso site: www.disaleditora.com.br

Vendas:
Televendas: (11) 3226-3111
Fax gratuito: 0800 7707 105/106
E-mail para pedidos: comercialdisal@disal.com.br

Table of Contents

Foreword

Dr. H. Douglas Brown, Ph.D. — Professor of English, San Francisco State University

It gives me great pleasure to offer this foreword to *English Pronunciation for Brazilians*. I have known the lead author, Sonia Godoy, since her student days at the University of Michigan in Ann Arbor, where she was a student in the Master of Arts program and I was her professor. I'm gratified to see that my own encouragement and Sonia's creativity have, with her co-authors Cris Gontow and Marcello Marcelino, given birth to this practical manual for students of English in Brazil. I'm very proud to see this accomplishment!

There are a number of characteristics of this book that I'm pleased to see. First, the book is for Brazilians and speaks directly to predictable phonological issues for Brazilian learners. There are many (maybe too many?) books in print that provide generic instruction in oral communication, not necessarily directed to any one group of native speakers. This book is appropriately targeted and speaks directly to its specified audience.

Second, the book is highly practical. Directions are easy to follow; exercises are clearly spelled out and are of interest and relevance to students. The material is simple and direct, and therefore does not risk going "over the heads" of students. And there is an ample amount of practice. In an era when some pedagogical trends incorrectly play down the importance of practice, this book stands out in its emphasis on practice for the psychomotor process of improving pronunciation.

Third, the material is student-centered and student-friendly. It forces students to take responsibility for their own learning with appropriate pair and group work activity — all of which is supported by an audio component that gives students an opportunity to hear models. The authors encourage students to self-monitor, which is a key strategic approach to the acquisition of phonological accuracy. And I like the student-friendly, humorous approach that enlivens what might otherwise be tedious practice.

Finally, I applaud the authors for their pedagogical approach to phonological acquisition. I have often used the analogy of "zooming in" as a strategy for all aspects of language learning — the occasional need to take a very close look at a language form. The authors effectively guide students to view broader contexts, to have a "close up" look, and to zoom in on details.

Congratulations to Sonia, Cris, and Marcello for an excellent achievement!

Preface

Welcome to *English Pronunciation for Brazilians – The Sounds of American English*. Unlike most books in the area, this pronunciation text does not aim at a worldwide market. It was **especially designed for speakers of Brazilian Portuguese**, and it relies on the authors' vast experience in teaching in Brazil to address all the areas of difficulty pertaining to this particular language group. Throughout the book, **English and Portuguese are contrasted**, guiding the students in transferring pronunciation habits. The body of the text focuses on the sounds of American English (vowels and consonants), and this variety was chosen as it is most commonly the one Brazilian students are interested in learning. This book was written for **intermediate to advanced** learners and although the focus is on general English, the abilities here acquired can easily be transferred to other settings to suit students' academic and/or professional needs. This textbook can be used with a **variety of learning formats**: large groups, small groups, private teaching and independent learning.

As discussed further in the book, **Brazilians in general have good pronunciation** when learning a foreign language. However, according to our personality or characteristics, we want to go **beyond intelligibility**, as most people want to sound as native-like as possible. This book provides enough practice **in foreign accent reduction**, introducing students to the pronunciation of English in North America as it is spoken by educated native speakers in fluent speech. Students are led to discover the principles of articulatory phonetics through experimenting with their own vocal tract. Theory is introduced and reinforced by numerous practice exercises working up from individual sounds and phrases to dialogs, meaningful guided practice and contextualized reading passages. A lot of the activities come in the form of **games and fun activities**. The idea is to ensure the carryover of pronunciation skills into real communication. Students will improve their ability to communicate in English, increasing substantially their **listening comprehension skills**.

The student-centered approach encourages peer and especially **self-monitoring**, an important element for self-improvement. The teacher will be a facilitator, encouraging learners to be active participants in changing their pronunciation habits. **Phonetic symbols** are taught in a light and fun fashion to enable students to check pronunciation in the dictionary, thus promoting **learner's independence**. The symbols are also important in demonstrating the difference between sounds and letters. Common spelling patterns are included, always having Brazilian Portuguese differences and interference in mind.

Humor, which is much in accordance with the personality of Brazilians in general, is a recurrent element that permeates the whole book. We believe that the use of humor helps students retain the sounds because they will tend to remember the tips and the conversations better.

Have fun! We know we did while writing this!

Sonia, Cris and Marcello

To the teacher

This textbook can be used with a variety of learning formats: large groups, small groups, private teaching and independent learning. The book provides a wide variety of activity types to stimulate students' interest and enjoyment in relation to pronunciation. There are a lot of **interactive activities** that you can adapt according to your needs.

Even though the authors believe the sequence of chapters presented in the book would work efficiently with most groups, you might want to follow a different sequence. For example, you might want to start with the vowels instead of the consonants. Just bear in mind that the authors had a progression in mind when they wrote the book, so follow the order suggested as much as possible.

High frequency vocabulary for intermediate to advanced students was used throughout the book, so refrain from spending class time explaining vocabulary. Students should be encouraged to look up unknown words in the dictionary if they have any doubts.

Remember that individuals vary a great deal in relation to their language abilities, especially pronunciation, and defining just what expectation your students have toward this course may help you guide them more successfully. A mismatch between teacher's goals and learners' expectations may generate a great deal of strain on the part of students, and pronunciation is supposed to be fun!

To the independent learner

If you are a student planning to work on your own, we understand that you have intermediate to advanced level of English. Even though the book is organized in chapters, you don't have to follow them in exactly that order. You may choose to start with "that sound you have always felt unsure of." Just bear in mind that the authors had a progression in mind when they wrote the book, so we recommend that you follow the order suggested as much as possible.

If you are taking a regular English course and decide to study pronunciation on your own in order to improve your English, talk to your teacher and ask for suggestions on which sounds you need to work more intensively. This should get you started all right!

One last word. Remember you are responsible for your own learning. Especially when dealing with pronunciation, it is very important that you constantly monitor yourself. We have taken every possible opportunity to remind you of that in the textbook, but the commitment has to come from you. Do the exercises over and over until you feel satisfied. You will see that your effort will pay off!

How To Use This Book

We believe that textbooks should be a safe haven for students to learn, where they can rely on a certain structure to guide them through their learning process. At the same time, we think that predictability, though comforting, can become boring at times. So we have tried, as much as possible, to follow a certain pattern within the units, but always trying to add an element of surprise, be it the humor with which some points are addressed or the variety of activities.

We have made the navigation in the book as simple as possible. The titles of the sessions are color coded to help identify when there is a change in the focus of the unit. An audio icon [ ] will show which material is recorded, and a pencil icon [ ] will indicate the exercises that require writing. The answers can be found in the Answer Key at the end of the book.

Every unit in the book will have the following sections. Here are some tips on how to go about them.

Section	Audio	Objective	Usual Procedure
Think About It	No	• To raise awareness of the differences between English and Portuguese sounds. • To discuss what you know about pronunciation and spelling rules. • To reflect on how you pronounce some troublesome words.	• Discuss the questions with classmates. • Pronounce the words as clearly as possible. • Don't check the Answer Key yet.
Close Up	Sometimes	• To describe the articulation of sounds in American English. • To contrast the pronunciation of English and Portuguese sounds.	• Go over this session carefully. There's important information there that shouldn't be skipped. • Check the meaning of the unknown technical words in the glossary at the end of the book.
Zoom In	Yes	• To practice the target sounds in words, phrases and sentences through repetition.	• Repeat the cues after the model. • Record your voice on a separate tape recorder if possible. Play back the recording and monitor yourself.
Get Your Tongue Around It	Yes	• To provide intensive practice of the articulation of sounds through different techniques. • To train your articulatory muscles enough so they will be able to perform correctly when needed.	• Listen to the whole activity and do it mentally first. • Listen again and do the activity out loud. • Repeat as many times as necessary until you are satisfied with your performance.

In Context	Yes	• To provide practice of the target sounds in paragraphs.	• Listen to the whole passage first. • Use the pause button to allow yourself enough time for repetition. • Close the book. Use the paragraph as a dictation exercise. Replay the paragraph sentence by sentence using the pause button.
Conversation	Yes	• To provide practice of the target sounds in words in dialogs.	• Listen to the whole passage first. • Use the pause button to allow yourself enough time for repetition. • Close the book and try to repeat sentence by sentence using the pause button.
Stay Tuned	Yes	• To work on sound discrimination.	• Listen to the recording and do the task provided.
Wrap Up	No	• To check your own progress. • To ensure you have understood the concepts addressed by the unit.	• Go back to Think About It and make sure you fully understand the answers to the questions. Look at the Answer Key to check your answers. If you still have doubts, go over the unit again.
Tip Boxes	Sometimes	• To call attention to interesting / important details.	• Read the tip and pronounce the words provided.
Glossary	No	• To define the technical terms used throughout the book.	• Use it when you come across a technical term you don't fully understand.
Audio Scripts & Answer Key	No	• To help students study independently.	• Check the Answer Key after you've finished the whole exercise. • Read the Audio Script only if necessary.

Part A
Pronouncing a Foreign Language

Intro – Some Thoughts on Pronunciation Teaching and Learning

In this book, you are going to find a lot more than formulas, techniques and tips on how to "pronounce English better." You are about to come face to face with new sounds, listening strategies, speech habits and even... attitude! Pronouncing a foreign language can be a challenge that involves a lot more than just knowing where to put your tongue!

Historical Facts: Three Views on Pronunciation Teaching

Without going into details, let's talk about the two major views on the teaching of pronunciation. There was once a belief that teaching pronunciation was to eradicate all traces of a foreign accent. The major focus was on specific sounds and the study of the contrast between the first language and English. The methodology used was based on repetition. The other view holds that teaching pronunciation to adult students is useless because older learners have difficulty in pronouncing certain sounds in a foreign language. This theory also claims that the only objective of learning a foreign language is to communicate, not to pronounce it perfectly, so everything should be OK if your listener is able to understand what you say. The direct consequence of this second view was that the study of pronunciation was nearly abandoned.

This is a book written by Brazilians for Brazilians, taking into consideration our specific needs, so we try to use what we consider to be the most effective aspects of the two views. Our own view of pronunciation learning is different from the views above, but it takes both into account. We believe in the importance of good pronunciation, and that it is possible to improve it.

Below we view some factors that influence the improvement of a person's pronunciation. You will see that you might be favored by some, and not by others – but hard work and motivation will help to even out the equation!

Influencing Factors

Biology

It is a fact that adults learning a second language almost always have a "foreign accent," while children who have been exposed to a second language from an early age almost always attain native-like pronunciation. If you think in terms of stretching, it becomes a little clearer. Imagine you are an adult who has never exercised in your life. If you started stretching today, you would not be as good as an athlete! It is the same with your mouth: it is made up of articulators and muscles that are used in certain movements – those of your native language. In learning a foreign language, you will have to move your articulators and stretch those muscles in a way they have never done before. While this is not impossible, it certainly requires a lot of willpower and dedication. Likewise, the final attainment of pronunciation by adults varies a great deal from one individual to another. And as much as we may try to deny it, this is definitely associated with the amount of practice and dedication... just like stretching!! Are you starting to get the idea behind this book? Let's stretch!!

The Role of the Native Language

After a certain age, a person's sound references are totally connected to the native language. It is almost as if the native language acted as a filter for any foreign sound. If the sound is identical, there is no problem. If the sound is different, it is reinterpreted according to the native sound system. For example, a beginning student who hears the pronunciation of the TH in English will find no corresponding sound in the Brazilian Portuguese system. The student's sound system will then reinterpret the sound according to the sounds it has and will approximate the TH to whatever sounds closer to it in Portuguese. That would bring the TH closer to /s/, /f/ or /t/, thus resulting in "sink," "fink" or "tink" instead of *think*. Likewise, some people might pronounce "day" instead of *they*. As a result, we could conclude that the native language affects not only the production of sounds but also the way a student hears them. For that reason, we believe that it is also important to focus on the listening skill when it comes to pronunciation. Learning pronunciation is learning to listen again! Production of the sounds comes almost as a by-product of good listening. Think about it: would we even speak our native language if we had not listened to it a lot?

The Brazilian Student Learning English: The Good News

Brazilians, in general, are considered to have good pronunciation in English. Are you surprised? Well, just compare our performance to Asian, German or Italian speakers. It's usually much easier for us. Why is that so? Some people claim that because Portuguese is not spoken in many countries, we are often exposed to different languages. This exposure would give us some training in picking up other languages.

Others will say that Portuguese is considered a rich language in terms of sounds. If we think of Spanish, for example, which is considered so close to Portuguese, we could point out some differences. It doesn't have the sounds /z/ or /ʒ/, which makes Spanish speakers say *cassa* instead of *casa* and ***ch**anela* instead of ***j**anela*. They also have problems telling apart /b/ and /v/. Spanish has just five vowel sounds: a, ê, i, ô, and u. These are a few examples of problems that we don't have to worry about. If you believe in that view, the Brazilian Portuguese variety and its richness give us extra ammunition to work with. None of that has been proved, however. It might just be the case that we Brazilians are more adaptable and open to learning and embracing other cultures and peoples. This more culturally oriented perspective would naturally result in embracing and accepting the new sounds of a foreign language like English. Whichever the hypothesis or rationale behind the facts, there is always room for improvement and we, Brazilians, do have a good starting point in terms of pronunciation!

Socio-Cultural Aspects

Have you ever asked yourself the following questions?

- Why am I studying English? Do I like it or do I just do it because I need it?
- How do I feel about the people from English speaking countries? Do I identify with their culture and traditions?
- Do I like the accent displayed on the audio material my teacher uses? Do I prefer British or American accent?

- Would I like to sound as a native speaker of English?
- What does it mean to speak with a native accent? How much of my identity would be lost if I started sounding like an American/British person?

As the questions above suggest, there are a number of things to be considered in the process of acquiring the pronunciation of English. Consider the following: if you moved to Porto Alegre or Portugal, would you be willing to change your pronunciation and speak like a Gaúcho or a Portuguese person? While you will suffer some influence whether you want it or not, how much your pronunciation will change depends on how much you identify with the language or accent in question. Your accent is a marker of your identity; it is part of who you are. How much of that are you willing to give up?

All these questions lead us to the distinction between ***accent*** and ***mispronunciation***. An accent is something that everybody, EVERYBODY has, whether they like it or not. It represents your roots and your history. You may have a native or a foreign accent. A native accent can be broken down into sub-accents: British, American, Jamaican, Australian, Scottish, etc. If it is American, it can be from the north, south, east or west. Take your pick. Think of Portuguese, it would be the same. Is your accent southern or northern? If it is southern, is it paulista, catarinense or carioca? How do you pronounce the word "poRta?"

Mispronunciation, on the other hand, is the distortion of the pronunciation of a word to an extent that it sounds either like another word or even incomprehensible to the listener. Mispronunciation can cause communication breakdowns. Do you know the meaning of the word "sôula?"[1]

Personality

Learners that are outgoing, confident and willing to take risks may be more likely to expose themselves to the foreign language and native speakers. This can be true at any level of practice, from speaking in the classroom and trying to imitate the sounds to talking to the native speakers you meet

1. This was a Russian trying to say "solo" in Portuguese. It was out of context, so everybody had a "question-mark" look on their faces: "sÔUla?"

socially. Remember that personality may play an important part in the way you see yourself pronouncing a foreign language. And by personality, we don't mean that shy people will necessarily have poor pronunciation, though their shyness might lead them to less exposure. **And exposure IS a determining factor for pronunciation improvement**.

Motivation

Motivation plays a vital role in ensuring success in the acquisition of good pronunciation. It does make a difference if you believe pronunciation is a very important part of language. Remember that change comes from within the individual, so in order for you to change your pronunciation, you have to WANT to change it. Don't be mislead by the popular belief that some people are born with a natural ability to learn languages and if you aren't one of them, you will never have good pronunciation. Research has shown that motivation is a much stronger factor than natural ability, so never allow yourself to get discouraged.

Your profile

Before you start your pronunciation studies, it is important for you to set your **goals**. We have devised a guide to encourage you to think about your needs and wants and help you (and possibly your teacher) meet those goals.

WHY I want to improve my pronunciation

We have listed some of the possible reasons why you want to improve your pronunciation. Check the ones that apply to you and feel free to add the ones that we have not included.

I want to improve my pronunciation because...

- I like English very much and think good pronunciation is important.
- I need to sound good enough to travel and to participate in informal conversations.
- I want to feel comfortable in videoconferences, telephone calls and business meetings.

- I give academic lectures or some other sort of formal presentations in English (and I want to be judged by my content, not by the way I speak.)
- I am or want to be an English teacher and I want to attain native-like proficiency.
- Others: ____
____

WHAT I want my pronunciation to be

Now is the time for you to start thinking about where you stand now and where you would like to be in the future. Pronunciation is a long-term skill to be acquired patiently. However, it is important to set your goals and go after them. But remember: they are not untouchable! You can always come back to this part of the book and reset your goals, because they might change in the course of this program. Below is a continuum that ranges from *heavy accent* to *native-like pronunciation*. Use a pencil and circle the point in the continuum where you think **you are now**. Then put an X at the point **you aim at**. Come back to this section at any time and change your goals according to your wants and needs. If you do that, use a different color so you see how your goal also changes as you go. It should be fun!

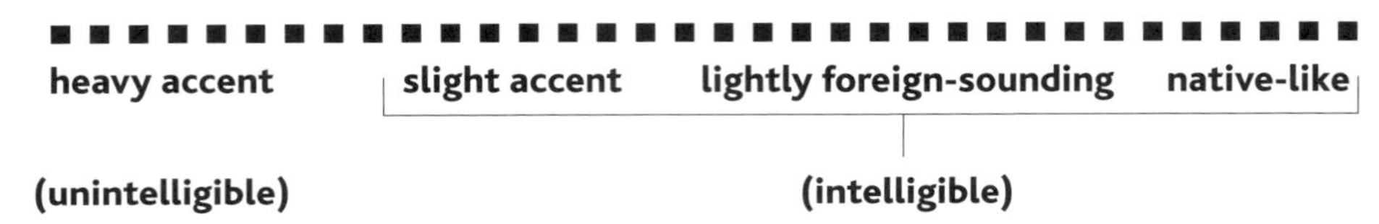

This book provides enough practice to help you go for any of the goals you decide on. Whatever your goal, however, remember that it depends a lot on yourself, your personality, your commitment, and exposure to English.

Any more benefits?

Studying pronunciation significantly influences the way you understand spoken English. Listening and pronunciation form a two-way street. You need to be able to discriminate sounds in order to produce them right. At the same time, once you learn how to pronounce a word correctly, you'll also be able to recognize it when you hear it. You will find that while your listening will improve, you'll also be more easily understood. Communicating then becomes a lot more comfortable in both directions.

Also, the fact that you are more aware of how things are supposed to sound will induce you to self-monitor, or develop that censorship system that will tell you when you mispronounce a word. **Self-monitoring is a determining factor for success**. No one but yourself will be standing next to you at all times to correct you.

A final word

While it is obvious that everybody can profit from studying pronunciation, there is an enormous difference in the attainment of good pronunciation from one learner to another. Remember: you may never be able to do a difficult yoga position but some stretching is always better and healthier than no stretching at all!! In language terms, this means you may not yet feel *"comfturble"* pronouncing a *"lotta"* the sounds you're *"gonna"* be exposed to in this book. Nevertheless, you WILL meet people who use those features of English and you need to be able to recognize them and understand them even though YOU don't *"hafta"* produce them yourself. Got it? Good luck!

Unit 1 – English x Portuguese

LA VIE EN ROSE - Adão Iturrusgarai

Think about it

In small groups, discuss these questions:

1. Have you ever seen a good English dictionary without indication of pronunciation? What about Portuguese dictionaries? Why (not)?
2. Do you think native speakers of English ever use the dictionary to check pronunciation?
3. Why do you think English students often study phonetic symbols?
4. Take a look at these words:

English	Portuguese
domicile	sufumigação
preface	tartarear
administrative	indenidade

Do you know what they mean? Do you know how to pronounce them? What's your conclusion? ____

____

Close up

When you look at the English words *domicile*, *preface* and *administrative*, you know what they mean, but you might not know how to pronounce them. On the other hand, when you look at the Portuguese words *sufumigação*, *tartarear* and *indenidade*, you probably have no idea what they mean, though you would have no problem pronouncing them.

Compare scenarios 1 and 2:

1. An American studying Portuguese
2. A Brazilian studying English

An American who is studying Portuguese can read out loud any word after learning the letter-sound correspondence, even if he/she doesn't know what the word means. That is, he won't have much trouble guessing which sound comes out of the combination of letters he/she sees. He might, however, have difficulty pronouncing the sound correctly. For example, he might not know what he has to do in order to pronounce ***não*** instead of ***nau***.

In scenario 2, on the other hand, things are quite different. Not only will the Brazilian student worry about which sounds come out of certain letter combinations, but many times he/she will also have to know ***how*** to articulate some of those sounds which do not exist in Portuguese. For example, when a Brazilian sees the words *ski* and *sky*, he/she might wonder: are they pronounced the same? What's the final sound, /i:/ or /aɪ/?

Zoom in

✎ Exercise 1: Match the columns rhyming the words:

1. b**ough**	( ) go
2. thr**ough**	( ) cup
3. alth**ough**	( ) true
4. b**ough**t	( ) cow
5. c**ough**	( ) cuff
6. hicc**ough** (old spelling)	( ) off
7. en**ough**	( ) caught

✎ Write your conclusion: ______________________________________

✎ Exercise 2: Write the number of sounds and letters in these two columns, as in the example. Note: diphthong (e.g. /aɪ/) = 1 sound

Portuguese			English		
word	letters	sounds	word	letters	sounds
bola	4	4	ball	4	3
imagine			imagine		
chocolate			chocolate		
diferente			different		
ai			eye		
fixa			ax		
Livia			leave		
arrastar			thought		

✎ What's your conclusion? ______________________________________

____

✎ Exercise 3. In Exercise 1, we saw that the same spelling can correspond to seven different sounds. On the other hand, the sound /i:/ as in t<u>ea</u> can have ***nine*** different spellings. Find an example for each of them:

ea ____________ ie ____________ i ____________
ee ____________ ei ____________ eo ____________
ey ____________ e ____________ oe ____________

Again, this poor relationship between spelling and sound doesn't happen in Portuguese. We Brazilians may have some trouble spelling out words (s or z // ss or ç // j or g), but we hardly have problems with knowing what to pronounce. That's not quite the same with native speakers of English. They occasionally use the dictionary to check the pronunciation of words in their own language. That's why English dictionaries show pronunciation and Portuguese dictionaries don't – it's not necessary. Portuguese is said to be a phonetic language, meaning that there is a good correspondence between spelling and sound. In English, however, this correspondence does not apply in such a clear-cut fashion.

Due to this characteristic of the English language, it's important for foreign students to learn phonetic symbols, as they'll often have to check pronunciation in the dictionary. Besides, as we will see, English has many more sounds than letters so the phonetic symbols are important to indicate these sounds.

Unit 2 – Developing Independence: Using the Dictionary to Check Pronunciation

Being able to check pronunciation in the dictionary means becoming independent: you can solve your pronunciation questions without having to ask anyone how to pronounce the words. However, you need some training. It's important to be familiarized with the dictionary you have, and to know the phonetic symbols it uses.

Think about it

Discuss these questions:

1. Have you ever used your dictionary to check pronunciation? Why? Why not?
2. Do all English dictionaries indicate pronunciation the same way?
3. Do you ever use the Pronunciation Key/Table in your dictionary when you check the pronunciation of a word?
4. You were probably in the first grade at school when you started learning how to separate syllables in Portuguese. Do you think the same happens in English?
5. Do you know how to separate syllables in English? Can people separate syllables in English easily? Why (not)?
6. Is it important to know exactly where a syllable starts and where it ends? How frequently do you need to use this knowledge?
7. Indicate the number of syllables the word *chocolate* has in

a. English: ___
b. Portuguese: ___

Close up

In Portuguese, the separation of syllables (syllabification) is mainly based on the sound (phonology). In English, morphology is also taken into account. In other words, how the words are formed plays an important role in how the syllables are divided. For example, the syllables in *teacher* are divided *teach-er*, separating the suffix. Take a look at the syllabification of these words:

every: ev-ery
memory: mem-o-ry
garbage: gar-bage
destroyed: de-stroyed
circumstance: cir-cum-stance
communism: com-mu-nis-m
chocolate: choco-late / choc-o-late

While some knowledge of morphology is required in order to divide syllables in English, no one needs to have it for this purpose, since syllable division is not common in English. Not even word processors are programmed to do that! The important thing is to know how many syllables a word has, and where the stress falls. And that is a much easier task to accomplish.

In Portuguese, the number of syllables a word has usually equals the number of vowel letters; that is, we practically pronounce all the letters we write. In English, the number of syllables equals the number of vowel ***sounds***, because we don't pronounce all the letters we write.

Zoom in

✎ Exercise 1: Write the number of syllables in these words.

stress	( )	smile	( )	rhythm	( )
airplanes	( )	through	( )	separate (adj.)	( )
like	( )	missed	( )	separate (verb.)	( )
Portuguese	( )	police	( )	advertisement	( )

Exercise 2: Compare and discuss your answers with a classmate and use a dictionary to check your answers.

2 Exercise 3: Now listen to the recording and repeat the words tapping your fingers at every syllable.

Exercise 4: It's important to be familiarized with ***your*** dictionary, so use it to do this exercise. Notice how it indicates syllable separation. Check the correct answer.

It separates syllables in
(   ) the dictionary entry (   ) the phonetic transcription

It uses
(   ) dots (   ) hyphens (   ) spaces

3 Exercise 5: The vowel is the nucleus of the syllable. Underline the **vowel** of the stressed syllable in the following words.

progress (n.)	politics	catholic
progress (v.)	political	contribute
democracy	politician	creative
independence	ignorance	develop

Listen to the recording, repeat the words and clap as you say the stressed syllable. Were your answers correct?

Close up

Many long words in American English have primary (most important) and secondary stress. Observe:

díctionàry	ùni**vér**sity
primary secondary	secondary primary

Zoom in

Different dictionaries show stress in different ways. Compare:

adolescent: /ˌædəlˈɛsənt/ - /ædəlɛsənt/ - /æd´əlɛs´ənt/

Look up the word *adolescent* in your dictionary and circle the notation that is similar to yours.

4 In British English, words ending in –ary/–ory have no secondary stress and have one less syllable.

	number of syllables	
	Am. E.	Br. E.
díctionary	4	3
sécretary	4	3
mándatory	4	3
dórmitory	4	3

In both cases, however, the primary stress falls on the same syllable.

Close up

Every dictionary has a **pronunciation key/table**. It brings the phonetic symbols followed by key words. Some also show how stress and syllabification are indicated. It's important to locate the key in your dictionary. It's usually at the beginning or at the end, and some dictionaries also have it on a separate slip.

Unit 3 – The Phonetic Alphabet

Think about it

Complete the chart in pairs. Write the numbers of letters and sounds each language has. Don't include nasal vowels or diphthongs.

	Brazilian Portuguese		American English	
	letters	sounds	letters	sounds
Vowels				
Consonants				

Close up

As said before, English has many more sounds than letters, so phonetic symbols are used to show these sounds. Study the chart:

	Brazilian Portuguese		American English	
	letters	sounds	letters	sounds
Vowels	5	7	5	12
Consonants	18	19	21	24

(Nasal vowels and diphthongs are not included.)

That's why phonetic symbols are important: to show pronunciation clearly, as the letter-sound correspondence is not as direct. Observe, for example, the fact that the letter ***o*** has a different sound in each of the following words:

m**o**re – n**o**te – c**o**me – l**o**t – t**o**mb – f**o**r (reduced form)
/ɔ/ /oʊ/ /ʌ/ /ɑ/ /u:/ /ə/

Some people say that phonetic symbols are difficult to learn. This is mainly because they vary from dictionary to dictionary, especially the vowels. The important thing is to be able to recognize the symbols used in ***your*** dictionary. Most English dictionaries use modified versions of the IPA (International Phonetic Alphabet).

Zoom in

Take a look at the **phonetic symbols for consonants** and corresponding key words.

1. /p/ - *p*et	13. /ʃ/ - *sh*e
2. /b/ - *b*oy	14. /ʒ/ - u*s*ual
3. /t/ - *t*ea	15. /tʃ/ - *ch*air
4. /d/ - *d*ay	16. /dʒ/ - *j*ust
5. /k/ - *c*ar	17. /m/ - *m*y
6. /g/ - *g*et	18. /n/ - *n*ight
7. /f/ - *f*our	19. /ŋ/ - ki*ng*
8. /v/ - *v*an	20. /l/ - *l*et
9. /θ/ - *th*ank	21. /r/ - *r*ed
10. /ð/ - *th*ey	22. /h/ - *h*ouse
11. /s/ - *s*ay	23. /w/ - *w*e
12. /z/ - *z*oo	24. /y/ - *y*es

Circle the unfamiliar symbols. How many unfamiliar symbols are there? What's your conclusion?

___

___

___

Close up

There are not so many new symbols to learn. Take a look at the unfamiliar symbols:

/θ/ and /ð/ both refer to "th." /θ/ is the sound in ***th***ink and au***th***or while /ð/ is the sound in ***th***at and mo***th***er.
/ʃ/ is usually written with "sh." It's the sound in ***sh***oes, ***sh***ow and ***sh***ine.
/tʃ/ is usually written with "ch." It's the sound in ***ch***eck, ***Ch***ina and ***ch***ur***ch***.
/ʒ/ is usually spelled "s" between vowels. It's the sound in mea***s***ure, ca***s***ual and plea***s***ure.
/dʒ/ is usually written with "j" or "g." It's the sound in ***j***ail, ***J***oe, ***G***eor***g***e and ***g***entleman.
/ŋ/ is usually written "ng" or "n" before /k/ and /g/. It's the sound in doi***ng***, lo***ng*** and tha***n***k.

Zoom In

✎ Even though all consonant sounds have their expected, typical spellings, it's important to notice there are atypical spellings as well. Match the columns below. Each number is going to be used twice. The first eleven items refer to the typical spelling, while the other eleven are less frequent.

1. /ʒ/	( ) ch	chair, cheap, much, search
2. /f/	( ) t or tt	ten, touch, sit, attention
3. /ʃ/	( ) s or ss ce, ci or cy	sad, bus, consider, sense, miss city, face, fence, decide, cycle
4. /w/	( ) z or zz	zero, dozen, size, buzz
5. /tʃ/	( ) sh	shop, fish, shut, ashamed
6. /dʒ/	( ) s	pleasure, usual, leisure, measure
7. /z/	( ) j g	jaw, enjoyment, subject, gentle, engine, cage, cottage
8. /g/	( ) k c or cc	take, kind, dark, call, scream, music, occur
9. /k/	( ) g or gg	go, glad, beg, biggest
10. /t/	( ) f or ff	from, foot, offer, soft

11. /s/	( ) w	wish, want, sweet, twist
	( ) ti ch ci si ssi x (/kʃ/) s or ss irregular	nation, attention, essential, ambitious machine, mustache, chic, Chicago, Michigan special, delicious, politician, suspicion comprehension, mansion, tension profession, expression, permission anxious, complexion sugar, sure, insurance, pressure conscious, ocean
	( ) gu x (/gz/)	guard, guess, vague exact, exist, examination
	( ) u irregular	quite, square, persuade, language one, once
	( ) sc x (/ks/)	scene, science, descend, discipline six, box, extra
	( ) ph gh	photograph, telephone laugh, cough, enough, rough, tough
	( ) s x (/gz/) ss	use (v.), nose, choose, buses exact, exist, examination possess, dissolve, dessert, scissors
	( ) dg d	edge, bridge, judge, knowledge gradual, soldier, during
	( ) si irregular	occasion, television, vision seizure, garage, genre, beige, luxurious
	( ) ed th	hoped, laughed, wished Thames, Thailand, Thomas, discotheque
	( ) tch tu ti	catch, stretch, kitchen nature, picture, lecture, future question, suggestion, digestion
	( ) ck qu ch x (/ks/) (/kʃ/)	back, luck, pocket quiet, equal, squeeze ache, stomach, chemistry six, box, extra anxious, complexion

Close up

Locate the pronunciation table/key in your dictionary. Complete the columns with the symbols and keywords your dictionary uses for the vowels.

	keywords	Most British Dictionaries / Books	Most American Dictionaries / Books	This Book	Your Dictionary	
					symbols	keywords
1	tea	iː	iy	iː		
2	big	ɪ	ɪ	ɪ		
3	pay	eɪ	ey	eɪ		
4	get	e	ɛ	ɛ		
5	cat	æ	æ	æ		
6	bar	ɑː	ɑ	ɑ		
7	about bird but	ə ɜː ʌ	ə ər / ɜr ʌ	ə ɜr ʌ		
8	not	ɒ	ɑ	ɑ		
9	four	ɔː	ɔ	ɔ		
10	go	əʊ	ow	oʊ		
11	book	ʊ	ʊ	ʊ		
12	blue	uː	uw	uː		
13	my	aɪ	ay	aɪ		
14	cow	aʊ	aw	aʊ		
15	boy	ɔɪ	ɔy	ɔɪ		

Now analyze this chart, comparing the symbols. Which system is more similar to the one your dictionary uses? ______________________________

It's very important to master the system in ***your*** dictionary. That's the one you're going to be referring to more frequently. Remember to use the pronunciation key/table. At the same time, it's also important to be able to recognize other common symbols used in other books and dictionaries.

Zoom in

Exercise 1: Practice using the symbols. Write the numbers from **zero to ten** under the appropriate symbol according to the vowel sound. Some of the numbers will go under two different symbols. Follow the example.

zero – one – two – three – four – five – six – seven – eight – nine – ten

/i:/	/ɪ/	/eɪ/	/ɛ/	/æ/	/ɑ/	/ʌ/	/ə/
zero							

/ɜr/	/ɔ/	/oʊ/	/ʊ/	/u:/	/aɪ/	/aʊ/	/ɔɪ/
		zero					

Exercise 2: Let's work with **colors**. Write the correct symbols between the bars. Refer to the vowel chart on the previous page. Use the key words to help you.

gr /   / n
bl /   / ck
bl /   /
p /   / nk
s /   / lv /   / r

wh /   / te
y /   / ll /   /
br /   / n
b /   / ge

r /   / d
p /   / p /   / l
g /   / ld
gr /   /

/fə'nætɪk fər fə'nɛtɪks/

What animals are these?

1. /'taɪgər/ ________
2. /kaʊ/ ________
3. /kæt/ ________
4. /bɜrd/ ________
5. /'tɜrki/ ________
6. /fɪʃ/ ________
7. /'tʃɪkən/ ________
8. /'ɛləfənt/ ________
9. /'zi:brə/ ________
10. /'kæməl/ ________
11. /'mʌŋki/ ________
12. /tʃɪmpæn'zi:/ ________
13. /ʃi:p/ ________
14. /'ræbɪt/ ________
15. /'laɪən/ ________
16. /'krɑkəˌdaɪl/ ________
17. /'ælɪˌgeɪtər/ ________
18. /dʒɪ'ræf/ ________

Fun time

In small groups, identify the transcriptions. Then choose the word that best completes each of the sentences below. The first group to finish it correctly is the winner.

1. /ə'proʊtʃ/	5. /tʃeɪndʒ/	9. /pi:s/	13. /'lʌvərz/
2. /'kætʃ/	6. /'kʌntri/	10. /'ɪŋglənd/	14. /θæŋk/
3. /'oʊpənd/	7. /'mʌðər/	11. /pu:l/	15. /pʊl/
4. /'yʊrəp/	8. /θɔt/	12. /aɪz/	16. /hɜrt/

a. It's hot. Let's enjoy the _____.
b. She _____ she had been invited.
c. Let's _____ clothes to the party.
d. He was _____ in the accident.
e. Look at my _____.
f. Hippies believed in love and _____.
g. He _____ the door.
h. Romeo and Juliet were young _____.
i. _____ the chair, please.
j. Brazil is a beautiful _____.
k. That's a good way to _____ the problem.
l. John Lennon was from _____.
m. We're planning a tour around _____.
n. Here. _____ the ball.
o. Does your _____ work as a teacher?
p. I'd like to _____ you for the money.

Unit 4 – Homophones and Homographs

Think about it

✎ Work individually. Then compare your answers with a partner.

1. How are these words pronounced?

tear	**live**
a. /tɛr/	a. /laɪv/
b. /tɪr/	b. /lɪv/

2. Identify the transcription:

a. /flaʊər/ ___________________________

b. /raɪt/ ___________________________

c. /seɪl/ ___________________________

d. /wɛr/ ___________________________

Don't look at the **Answer Key** now! Study the unit to the end and then check your answers.

Close up

Homophones are words that have different spelling but sound the same:

heel } /hi:l/
heal }

Homographs are words that have the same spelling but two different pronunciations:

read } /ri:d/ - present
read } /rɛd/ - past

Zoom in

Exercise 1: Complete the charts with homophones and homographs in English and in Portuguese. Find four examples for each.

HOMOGRAPHS (= spelling **but** ≠ sound)

English:		

Portuguese:	*colher (pick up) / colher (spoon)*	

HOMOPHONES (= sound **but** ≠ spelling)

English:		

Portuguese:		

Could you think of as many homophones and homographs in English as in Portuguese?

Why do you think that happens? ____________________

/fəˈnætɪk fər fəˈnɛtiks/

✎ Identify the homophones. Work individually first. Then compare with a partner.

/si:/: *see / sea*
/ˈflaʊər/: ________ ________
/roʊd/: ________ ________
/wʊd/: ________ ________
/bɔrd/: ________ ________
/ˈhaɪər/: ________ ________
/pæst/: ________ ________
/ˈwɛðər/: ________ ________
/bɛr/: ________ ________
/weɪ/: ________ ________
/hi:l/: ________ ________
/breɪk/: ________ ________
/sɛl/: ________ ________

/meɪl/: ________ ________
/fɛr/: ________ ________
/meɪd/: ________ ________
/noʊ/: ________ ________
/ðɛr/: ______ ______ ______
/mi:t/: ________ ________
/saɪt/: ______ ______ ______
/wɛr/: ________ ________
/baɪ/: ______ ______ ______
/pi:s/: ________ ________
/daɪ/: ________ ________
/kru:z/: ________ ________
/hu:z/: ________ ________

Fun time

✎ This is a newspaper ad. The person who wrote is not a good speller and confused some words. Can you write them correctly?

BIG SAIL HEAR AT MEYER'S & SUN

SHOES: BY SUM NICE PEARS FOUR JUST ATE DOLLARS

CLOSE: THE HOLE STOCK ON SAIL WITH SPECIAL PRICES. SEA THE VARIETY OF COLORS WE OFFER: YELLOW, READ, PINK AND BLEW

DON'T WEIGHT! TOO WEAKS ONLY! BEE OUR SPECIAL GUESSED.

OPENING OURS: FROM ATE TWO FOR (ON SATURDAY WE CLOTHES AT WON.)

KNEW ADDRESS: 36 KING RODE

Part B
The English Consonants

Intro – The Organs of Speech and the English Consonants

Open your mouth and articulate a palatal fricative.

Think about it!

✎ Mark the correct answers.

1. We use the __________ air stream to speak.
   ( ) ingressive (in-coming)
   ( ) egressive (outgoing)

2. These are the organs of speech.

( ) stomach	( ) pharynx	( ) nose
( ) lungs	( ) larynx	( ) ear
( ) trachea	( ) mouth	

3. When we breathe in, our vocal folds[1] are
   ( ) completely open
   ( ) half open
   ( ) completely closed

✎ Write *True* or *False*.

1. All vowels are produced with the vibration of our vocal folds, that is, all vowels are voiced. ( )
2. All consonants are produced with the vibration of our vocal folds. ( )
3. Most English sounds are voiceless (produced without the vibration of the vocal folds. ( )

Don't look at the **Answer Key** now! Study the unit to the end and then check your answers.

1. Some phoneticians still refer to them as "vocal cords."

Close up

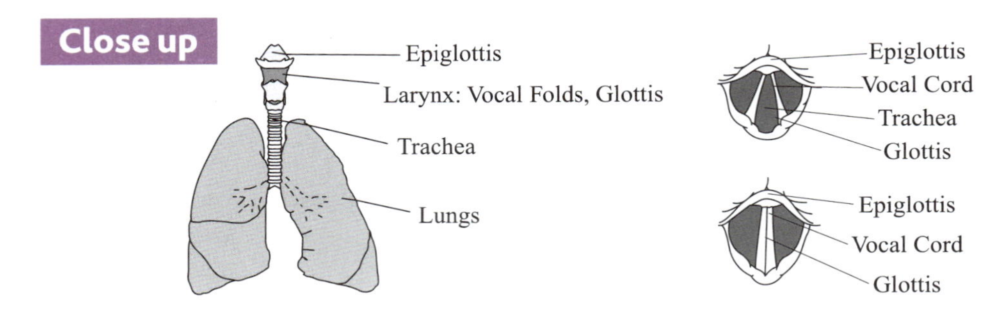

The air leaving the lungs will go through the trachea (wind pipe) and vibrate or not the vocal folds located in the larynx (voice box). Then it will leave through your mouth and/or nose.

The vocal folds open completely to allow the air in when we breathe in. When we breathe out, two things can happen:

- If we're not speaking, our glottis (the space between our vocal folds) will be open and the air flows freely.
- If we're speaking, our vocal folds come together allowing a narrow passage for the air to go out.

If the vocal folds vibrate when the air leaves, we produce a ***voiced*** sound. If they don't, we produce a ***voiceless*** sound. It's the case of the consonants: some are voiceless while some are voiced. However, all vowels are voiced, that is, the vocal folds always vibrate when we produce a vowel sound. Most consonants are voiced: English has only nine voiceless sounds.

To feel this vibration, put your fingertips against your Adam's apple (i.e., larynx) or on the top of your head and alternate these sounds:

ssss – zzzz – ssss – zzzz

You can feel the voicing turn **on** and **off**: /s/ is voiceless and /z/ is voiced.

Zoom in

✎ Touch your larynx or put your hand on top of your head and pronounce the following sounds. Circle VL if the sound is voiceless (no vibration) or VD if the sound is voiced (vibration).

/f/ VL VD /ʃ/ VL VD
/v/ VL VD /ʒ/ VL VD

Close up

MANNER AND PLACE OF ARTICULATION OF THE ENGLISH CONSONANTS									
			bilabial	labiodental	dental	alveolar	palatal	velar	glottal
Stops: breath is fully stopped and then released		Voiceless	/p/			/t/		/k/	[ʔ][1]
		Voiced	/b/			/d/		/g/	
Fricatives: breath causes friction		Voiceless		/f/	/θ/	/s/	/ʃ/		/h/
		Voiced		/v/	/ð/	/z/	/ʒ/		
Affricates: breath is stopped and friction follows		Voiceless				/tʃ/			
		Voiced				/dʒ/			
Nasals: breath is released through the nose		Voiced	/m/			/n/		/ŋ/	
Liquids: breath does not cause friction	lateral	Voiced				/l/			
	retroflex					/r/			
	flap					[ɾ][2]			
Semivowels: mouth moves from one position to another		Voiced	/w/				/y/		

1. The symbol [ʔ] refers to a sound that can sometimes replace /t/. Example: that you know /ðæʔ yu: noʊ/.
2. When Americans say *water* and lady, the “t” and “d” are usually pronounced [ɾ]. Example: better /ˈbɛɾər/ - metal /ˈmɛɾəl/

Zoom in

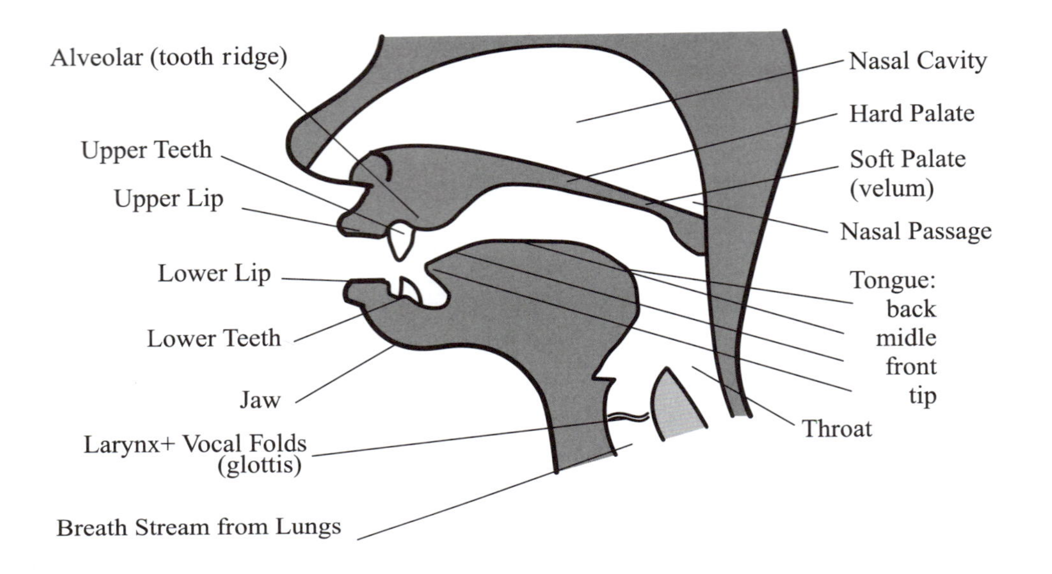

Complete the statements below...

- analyzing the consonant chart;
- observing what you do with your mouth as you pronounce each sound;
- and looking at the illustration above.

1. ***Bilabial*** sounds are produced with both ________________.
2. ***Labiodental*** sounds are produced with the upper ________________ and lower ________________.
3. ***Dental*** sounds are produced with the tip of your tongue between your ________________.
4. ***Alveolar*** sounds are produced with the tip of your ________________ approaching or touching the tooth ridge.
5. ***Palatal*** sounds are produced with your ________________ near the hard palate.
6. ***Velar*** sounds are produced with your tongue near or on the soft ______ __________, also called *velum*.
7. ***Glottal*** sounds are produced by ________________ passing through or stopping at your vocal ________________.

Unit 1 – /θ/ and /ð/

Think about it

Most students know that Portuguese does not have the "th" sound. What many people don't know is that there are two "th" sounds in English. One of them is voiced and the other is voiceless. An easy way to identify if the sound is voiceless or voiced is the following:

- If the "th" is similar to /f/, /t/ or /s/, it's voiceless (/θ/).
- If it's similar to /v/, /d/ or /z/, it's voiced (/ð/).

✎ Circle the "th" sound in these words:

1.	they	/θ/	/ð/	4.	either	/θ/	/ð/
2.	thought	/θ/	/ð/	5.	theater	/θ/	/ð/
3.	although	/θ/	/ð/	6.	north	/θ/	/ð/

Pronounce the words above. Do you put your tongue between your teeth every time /θ/ or /ð/ occurs?

Don't look at the **Answer Key** now! Study the unit to the end and then check your answers.

Close up

Let's produce the voiceless "th" /θ/. Say a long /s/: /ssss/. Your tongue approaches the back part of your upper teeth. Now say /s/, but put your tongue between your teeth. Say the sentence *Cida sabe sambar* as if you had a lisp ("língua presa"). This is the /θ/ sound.

Zoom in

5 Exercise 1: Repeat these words.

thank – **th**ousand – **th**ief – **th**ree
some**th**ing – any**th**ing – every**th**ing
nor**th** – ba**th** – mou**th** – bir**th**

6 Exercise 2: Listen to these cues and respond with a /θ/ word. Don't read the cues if you can! Follow the example:

Model: 2 + 1
You: Three
Model: Three

1. a day of the week
2. not fat
3. a school subject
4. you have them in your mouth
5. not south
6. 40 – 10
7. a sports professional
8. past of think
9. you use it to speak and eat
10. he who writes a book

In pairs, write five riddles with /θ/ like the ones above. Work with another pair. Guess each other's riddles.

In context

7 Listen to this paragraph.

Three **th**in **th**ieves **th**ought it was possible to come in **th**rough the ba**th**room window. **Th**ief number one **th**rew **th**e rope and climbed up; **th**ief number two told number **th**ree to count to **th**irty and let go. **Th**ief number **th**ree didn't know his ma**th**, counted to **th**irteen instead, and bo**th** fell into some **th**orny bushes below.

Repeat the paragraph pausing the recording.

Fun time

Look at the pictures above and answer these questions as in the example. Pay attention to the /θ/ sound in the ordinal numbers!

Who is the tallest?
The fourth one.

Who is the oldest?
Who wears glasses?
Who is the oddest?

Who has long hair?
Who is the heaviest?
Who is the shortest?

Can you come up with more questions?

Get your tongue around it

8 Exercise 1: Repeat linking the sounds.

truth or lie
both of us
a birth announcement

a math evaluation
north and south
growth impediment

health insurance
wrath of gods
wealth and wisdom

> 9 The "th" in these words is pronounced /t/.
> **Th**omas – **Th**ames – **Th**ailand – **Th**ompson – disco**th**eque

Work in pairs and check your friend's pronunciation.

10 Exercise 2: Compare these words. Listen and repeat.

initial /s/ x /θ/	initial /t/ x /θ/	initial /f/ x /θ/
sank – **th**ank	tree – **th**ree	fought – **th**ought
sink – **th**ink	tick – **th**ick	fret – **th**reat
sin – **th**in	true – **th**rough	free – **th**ree

final /s/ x /θ/	final /t/ x /θ/	final /f/ x /θ/
mass – ma**th**	tent – ten**th**	oaf – oa**th**
pass – pa**th**	Matt – ma**th**	deaf – dea**th**
mouse – mou**th**	boot – boo**th**	miff – my**th**

Stay tuned

11 Listen to these sentences and choose the correct picture.

Think about it

Say the past tense of the verb *dar* in Portuguese: *dei*. Now say the English word *they*. Do they sound the same or different?

Pronounce these words.

this	al**th**ough	brea**the**
these	wea**th**er	ba**the**
though	fa**th**er	wi**th** *

Did you place your tongue correctly to pronounce the "th?"

* In some varieties of English, *with* and *without* are pronounced with /θ/.

Close up

Let's practice the voiced "th" /ð/. Say a long /z/: /zzzz/. Your tongue approaches the tooth ridge. Now say /z/, but put your tongue *between* your teeth. Try to say the sentence *A casa da zebra é azul* as if you had a lisp ("língua presa"). That is the /ð/ sound. When you say the word *dei*, the tip of your tongue touches the area right behind your upper teeth, while when you say *they* your tongue is between your teeth.

Zoom in

12 Exercise 1: Repeat these words putting the tip of your tongue between your teeth.

o**th**er – ra**th**er – **th**em – **th**eir – **th**ey – **th**ough
ei**th**er – nei**th**er – wi**th**out – lea**th**er

13 Exercise 2: Repeat these sentences.

My mo**th**er is going to ba**th**e my bro**th**er.
Let's brea**th**e toge**th**er.
This, **th**at, **th**ese and **th**ose are pronouns.
My fa**th**er hopes my bro**th**er will tee**th**e soon.

14 Exercise 3: Compare these words. Pay attention to the fact that the second word is always pronounced with the tongue between your teeth.

/d/ /ð/
day – **th**ey
dough – **th**ough
doze – **th**ose
den – **th**en
dare – **th**ere

Stay tuned

15 Listen to these words and circle the sound you hear.

1. /d/ /ð/
2. /d/ /ð/
3. /d/ /ð/
4. /d/ /ð/
5. /d/ /ð/
6. /d/ /ð/
7. /d/ /ð/
8. /d/ /ð/
9. /d/ /ð/
10. /d/ /ð/

Get your tongue around it

16 Repeat these phrases, linking the sounds.

brea**the** in
brea**the** out
ba**the** Ellen
ba**the** Adam
wi**th** attention
wi**th** envy

In context

17 Close your book and listen to this paragraph. How many times was /ð/ pronounced?

These are my mo**th**er, my fa**th**er and my bro**th**er. Al**th**ough **th**ey don't look like me, **th**ere are many ways in which we are similar. **Th**ey are trustwor**thy** and **th**ey never tell each o**th**er lies. Clo**th**ing is ra**th**er unimportant to **th**em, as **th**ey believe it's what's inside **th**at counts. And **the** best of all, **th**ey live in ano**th**er country, so **th**ere is no way we can bo**th**er each o**th**er!

Repeat the paragraph after the model.

Zoom in

18 Compare these words:

/θ/	/ð/
teeth	to teethe
mouth	to mouth
thigh	thy
ether	either
north	northern

19 The vowel sounds in these words are also different.
south /saʊθ/ – southern /ˈsʌðərn/
breath /brɛθ/ – breathe /bri:ð/

/fəˈnætɪk fər fəˈnɛtɪks/

Match the words and their transcription:

1. ether
2. thigh
3. though
4. thief
5. teeth
6. they
7. either
8. those
9. thought
10. this

a. ___/ðeɪ/
b. ___/θi:f/
c. ___/ðɪs/
d. ___/ðoʊ/
e. ___/θɔt/
f. ___/ti:θ/
g. ___/ðoʊz/
h. ___/ˈi:θər/
i. ___/ˈi:ðər/
j. ___/θaɪ/

Fun time

✎ Let's play ***Categories***! Get into groups. Find one "th" word to fit each category. You get 5 points if you finish first and one extra point for each word pronounced correctly.

Categories

an ordinal number: ______________________
a quality: ______________________
a demonstrative pronoun: ______________________
a part of the house: ______________________
a material: ______________________
a noise from nature: ______________________
a preposition: ______________________
a family member: ______________________
a name: ______________________
a part of the body: ______________________
a profession: ______________________
a public building: ______________________

Wrap up

Go back to **Think about it** on page 51 and go over the questions again. Then check your answers in the **Answer Key**.

Unit 2
Final Nasals: /m/, /n/ and /ŋ/

Think about it

Does Portuguese have /m/ in final position? Do you think Brazilians have problems with this sound at the end of a word or syllable?

Pronounce these words.

ho**me**	co**m**fortable
gu**m**	so**me**thing
zoo**m**	crea**m**
ga**me**	la**mb**

Did you close your lips every time the /m/ occurred?

Close up

The nasal /m/ doesn't occur in final position in Portuguese at all. Words such as *também* and *sem* are written with a final **m** but are pronounced with a final nasal diphthong /ẽi/.

Let's contrast: *cantaram* and *cantarão*. The only real difference is the stress: *cant**á**ram* and *cantar**ão***. The final sound is the same nasal diphthong: /ão/. There is no bilabial movement. Pronounce the word *my*. Do you notice your lips touch? Now observe your lips when you say: *cantaram*. They don't touch at the end, as they would for an /m/ sound.

Zoom in

20 Exercise 1: Listen to these words. The /m/ always has the sound of *m* in *my*.

ai**m** – co**me** – Ro**me** – th**em** – so**me** – To**m**

21 Exercise 2: Repeat these words with /m/ at the end of a word or syllable, making a bilabial movement (touching your lips) at the end. Pay attention to the model.

syste**m** – drea**m** – co**m**fortable – ca**m**corder
na**me** – rhy**me** – chi**m**ney – di**me**

Now read the words in pairs, observing each other's mouths. Add some more words to the lists.

22 Exercise 3: Repeat these sentences with the words from **Think about it**.

My **home** is **comfortable**.
Chewing **gum** is **something** I hate.
Use the **zoom** in order to see the **game**.
The **lamb** was eating the **cream**.

Get your tongue around it

23 Listen to the words and put them in the correct place in the sentence. Remember to link the sounds. Follow the example.

Model: *Sam is my friend.*
You : *Sam is my friend.*
Model: *Jim*
You: *Jim is my friend.*
Model: *here*
You: *Jim is here.*

> Observe how this is really pronounced:
> Ji-miz-my-friend.
> Ji-miz-here.

Do it mentally (in silence) first. Then play the track again and do it orally.

In context

24 Exercise 1: Repeat linking the sounds:

drea**m** of	Coliseu**m** in	cal**m** and	li**me** ice crea**m**
Ro**me** in	atriu**m** of	consu**me** a lot	crea**m** and

25 Exercise 2: Listen to this paragraph.

I drea**m** of taking **my** ca**m**corder to Ro**me** in the autu**mn** to fil**m** the Coliseu**m** in Nove**m**ber. Fro**m** the atriu**m** of **my** hotel I would exa**m**ine the custo**m**s of the Ro**m**ans. How cal**m** and co**m**posed I would beco**me**! I would consu**me** a lot of li**me** ice crea**m** and just enjoy life.

Repeat the paragraph pausing the recording. Remember to link the sounds.

26 The Silent Corner

The letters ***n*** and ***b*** are silent in the following words, so the final sound is /m/. Listen and repeat:

silent n:
hym~~n~~ – dam~~n~~ – colum~~n~~ – autum~~n~~

silent b:
com~~b~~ – bom~~b~~ – lam~~b~~ – tom~~b~~ – crum~~b~~ – dum~~b~~
clim~~b~~ – num~~b~~ – thum~~b~~

Attention to the pronunciation: tomb /tu:m/

Conversation

27 Jim and Tom are archeologists. Listen to their conversation and cross out the silent letters.

Jim: To**m**, we have a proble**m**: we have to bo**mb** the colu**mn** or we won't be able to get into the to**mb**.

Tom: Ji**m**! We have to co**mb** the field before we bo**mb** it, or the walls will go to cru**mb**s and we might destroy so**me**thing i**m**portant.

Jim: OK, To**m**.

Practice the conversation in pairs.

Think about it

Say slowly "no, no, no." Observe the point your tongue touches inside your mouth: the area just behind your upper front teeth. Now say the Portuguese words *hífen – inveja – ensino*. Does your tongue touch that area when you pronounce the "n?" Do we have /n/ at the end of a word or syllable in Portuguese?

Pronounce these words.

pho**ne**	co**n**versatio**n**
o**ne**	o**n**ly
u**n**happy	trai**n**

Did your tongue touch the area just behind your upper front teeth every time the /n/ occurred?

Close up

The nasal /n/ doesn't occur in final position in Portuguese. The /n/ at the end of a syllable or word in Portuguese usually nasalizes the preceding vowel, but it is not articulated as a consonant. For example, in the word *inseto*, we don't pronounce *i* + *n*, but a nasal *i*. In English, the "n" always has the value of /n/ as in *no*, and every time you say it, the tip of your tongue has to touch the area just behind your upper front teeth.

Zoom in

28 Repeat these words putting your tongue on the tooth ridge.

su**n** – fi**n**e – Ja**n**e – agai**n** – i**n**sa**n**e – gree**n**

The **e** is silent in *Jane*, *fine* and *insane*, so we have a final /n/.

Get your tongue around it

29 Exercise 1: Repeat linking the sounds:

a**n** old ma**n** i**n** white
baco**n** a**n**(d) eggs
agai**n** a**n**(d) agai**n**

a**n** easy lesso**n** i**n** Arabic
a coi**n** of te**n**
a spoo**n** of cor**n** oil

i**n** a**n**(d) out
the su**n** and the moo**n**
fi**ne** arts

In pairs, make sentences using the expressions above.

30 Exercise 2: Ben loves the number seven. He has seven of everything! Substitute the words as in the example:

Model: art books
You: *Ben has seven art books.*
Model: armchairs
You: *Ben has seven armchairs.*

Now you do it.

In context

31 Repeat these proverbs after the model.

A ma**n** is know**n** by his frie**n**ds.
As soo**n** as a ma**n** is bor**n** he begi**n**s to die.
A frie**n**d **in** **n**eed is a frie**n**d **in**deed.
No ma**n** is i**n**dispe**n**sable.
No pai**n**, **n**o gai**n**.
One ma**n**'s loss is a**n**other ma**n**'s gai**n**.

Read each proverb aloud and say if you agree with it.

Remember: This is what you really say.
A man is = A-ma-niz
As soon as = a-soo-naz

Zoom in

32 Exercise 1: Students sometimes have problems pronouncing /eɪ + n/. Pay attention not to say /ɛ/ as in *get*. Listen and repeat.

pl**ane**/pl**ain**	m**ain**/m**ane**	tr**ain**
Sp**ain**	ch**an**ge	d**an**ger
compl**ain**	m**ain**t**ain**	expl**ain**
r**ain**	ins**ane**	**an**gel

33 Exercise 2: Repeat this sentence from the movie *My Fair Lady*.

Make sentences using the words in exercise 1 as the example in the balloon.

Close up

Say these words in Portuguese: *manga – banco*. Now just say the first syllable and hold the last sound: maŋŋŋ, baŋŋŋ...When the "n" is followed by "k" or "g," it's pronounced /ŋ/. The "g" in final position is NOT pronounced!

Zoom in

34 Exercise 1: Listen and repeat the contrasting words.

su**n**/so**n** – su**ng** – su**n**k ba**n** – ba**ng** – ba**n**k ra**n** – ra**ng** – ra**n**k
thi**n** – thi**ng** – thi**n**k do**n**e – du**ng** – du**n**k wi**n** – wi**ng** – wi**n**k

35 Exercise 2: Can you hear the difference between the two "n's?" Repeat:

sin a lot ran up win a fortune
sing a lot rang up wing of fortune

In context

36 Listen to the paragraph with books closed. In pairs, retell the story.

The ki**ng** ran as if he had wi**ng**s when the telephone ra**ng**. The queen was traveli**ng** to a neighbori**ng** ki**ng**dom, and the ki**ng** missed her tremendously. The ki**ng** was tha**n**kful she called. It was a most unhappy conversation, though, as the queen had fallen in love with the you**ng** prince and she was thinki**ng** of livi**ng** in his toweri**ng** castle. The ki**ng** moaned and groaned, but the queen did not return to his ki**ng**dom.

Repeat the paragraph pausing the recording.

37 Notice the difference:

singer	finger	ginger
/ˈsɪŋər/	/ˈfɪŋgər/	/ˈdʒɪndʒər/

The /g/ is **not** pronounced when you have verb + suffix:
hanger, singer, longing, banging, bringing

In other cases, the "g" is pronounced:

/g/	/dʒ/
anger	stranger
longer	plunger
hunger	challenger
stronger	danger

Zoom in

38 Exercise 1: When /n/ follows /t/ or /d/ in an unstressed syllable, no vowel sound is produced. However, it still counts as a separate syllable. Listen.

eate**n** /ˈi:tn̩/	writte**n** /ˈrɪtn̩/	gotte**n** /ˈgɑtn̩/
garde**n** /ˈgɑrdn̩/	pardo**n** /ˈpɑrdn̩/	did**n**'t /ˈdɪdn̩t/

This sound is called ***syllabic /n/*** (bitten /ˈbɪtn̩/). In this case, /t/ and /d/ are usually released through the nose. You don't have to produce the syllabic /n/, but you have to be able to recognize it.

39 Exercise 2: Repeat this sentence.

He could**n**'t find the butto**n** hidde**n** in the garde**n**.

/fəˈnætɪk fər fəˈnɛtɪks/

Match the sentences and the pictures.

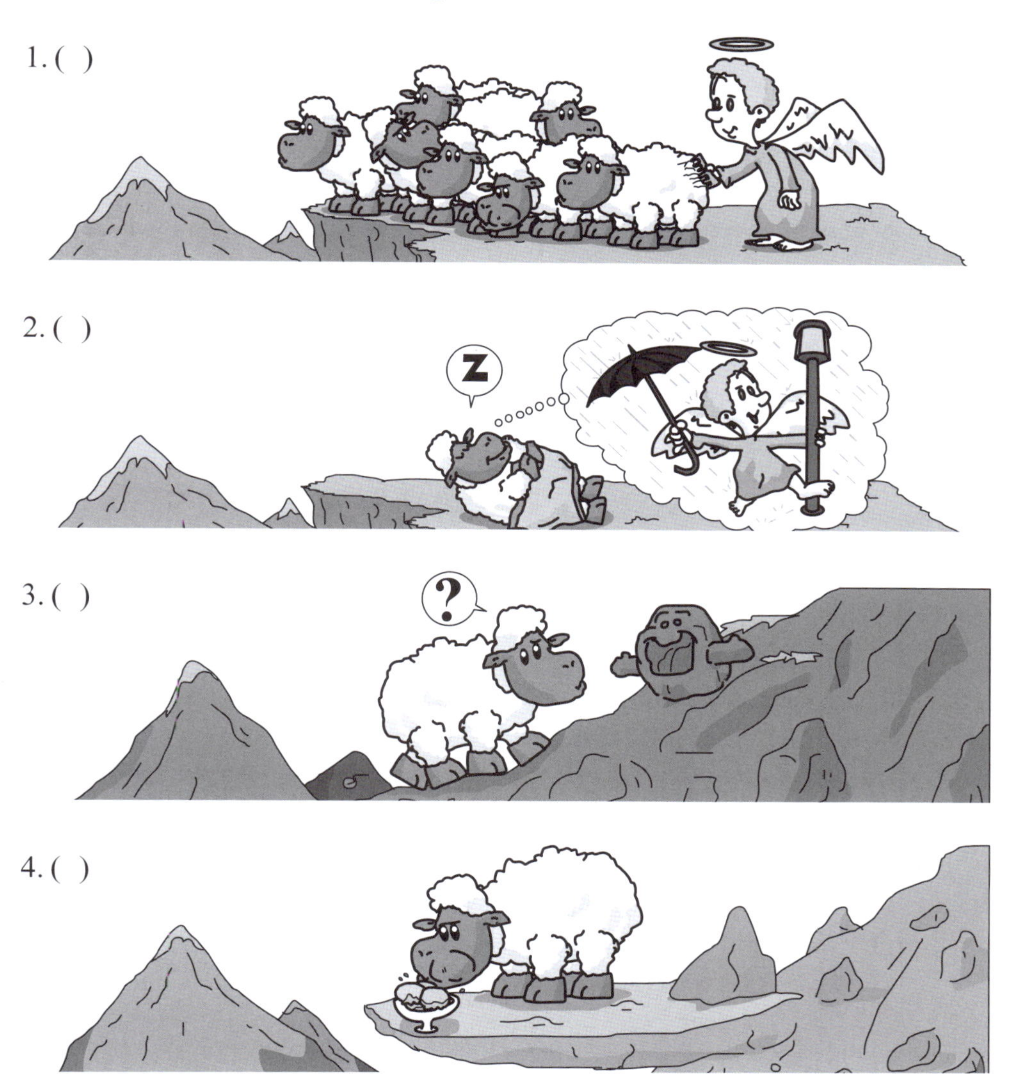

a. /ðə læm klaɪmd ðə ˈmaʊntn̩ ənd faʊnd ˈsʌmθɪŋ streɪndʒ/
b. /wʌn kyu:t læm dri:md əv ən ˈeɪndʒəl ˈkɑmli ˈsɪŋɪŋ ɪn ðə reɪn/
c. /ə ˈtʃɑrmɪŋ læm wəz ˈi:tɪŋ aɪs kri:m ɑn ðə ˈdeɪndʒrəs rɪm əv ðə ˈmaʊntn̩/
d. /ðɪ ˈeɪndʒəl wəz ˈkoʊmɪŋ ˈsɛvən læmz ɑn ðə ˈmaʊntn̩/

Fun time

Play *A Marvelous Nasal Story*. Here are the instructions:

- Get into groups of three or four. Each player should have a marker.
- The first player chooses any word and starts a story. The next player has to choose another word and continue the story.
- When the player pronounces the word correctly, he/she crosses it and moves the corresponding number of squares on the board.
- If a player mispronounces the word, he/she goes back the same number of squares.
- The winner is the first player to get to FINISH and to end the story.

START

FINISH

1 square
arm | time | coming
thing | thing | fun | woman
| home | king | thin

2 squares
train | going | dame
firm | anything | Spain
queen | ring | storm

3 squares
chimney | something
wing | win | bringing
Hamlet | lamb
done | van

4 squares
singing | climb | clumsy
gaining | gymnasium
hanging | insane
tongue | cane

Unit 3 - /r/ and /h/

Think about it

Compare:
Case 1:

Portuguese	English
humor	humor
herói	hero
helicóptero	helicopter
horrível	horrible
hilário	hilarious

What about…
Case 2:

Portuguese	English
honesto	honest
hora	hour

What happens to the "h" in Portuguese? What conclusions can you reach regarding the pronunciation of "h" in English? Which case is more frequent?

Close up

Close your nose and breathe out: /h.../. That's the /h/ sound. For some Brazilians, depending on the idiolect, these words may sound the same:

English	Portuguese
hey/hay	rei
he	ri

Because of this similarity, a lot of Brazilians have problems differentiating /h/ and /r/ in English. The initial /h/ in Portuguese is silent, whereas in English it is usually pronounced.

Zoom in

40 Exercise 1: Repeat these words:

hi – **h**ouse – **h**ill – **h**air – **h**eaven – **h**ello
un**h**appy – over**h**ead – in**h**abitant – in**h**erit

41 Exercise 2: Repeat these sentences:

The **h**appy **h**ippie **h**ad **h**orrible **h**air.
The in**h**abitant of New **H**ampshire **h**ad never **h**ad **h**am and eggs before.
There's a **h**orrid **h**aunted **h**ouse on the **h**ill.
In **H**artford, **H**ereford and **H**ampshire, **h**urricanes **h**ardly ever **h**appen[2].

2. From *My Fair Lady*

42 The Silent Corner

The "h" is silent in the following words. Listen and repeat:

~~h~~our – ~~h~~eir – ~~h~~onor – ~~h~~onest – ex~~h~~ibit – ex~~h~~ibition – ve~~h~~icle

Possible pronunciation for:
herb /ɜrb/ or /hɜrb/
human /ˈyu:mən/ or /ˈhyu:mən/

43 Exercise 2: Repeat these sentences:

An honest man waited for an hour.
An heir is an honorable guest.

Before these words, use the article "an." Compare:
a helicopter
an ~~h~~our

Get your tongue around it

Compare these words:

ear	–	**h**ear/**h**ere
ill	–	**h**ill
it	–	**h**it
am	–	**h**am
eye/I	–	**h**i
eight/ate	–	**h**ate

44 Repeat the pairs of words above.

/fəˈnætɪk fər fəˈnɛtɪks/

Match the words and the transcriptions.

1.	honest	a.	___/əgˈzɪbɪt/
2.	homeless	b.	___/vɪˈhɪkyələr/
3.	exhibit	c.	___/ˈɑnəst/
4.	exhale	d.	___/ˈhʌni/
5.	honorable	e.	___/ɛr/
6.	honey	f.	___/ˈɑnərəbl/
7.	vehicle	g.	___/hɛr/
8.	vehicular	h.	___/ˈhoʊmləs/
9.	heir	i	___/ˈvi:əkəl/
10.	hair	j	___/ˈɛksheɪl/

In context

45 Repeat the paragraph after the model, and then practice it in pairs.

Hugh and **H**arry are **h**umorists from **H**olland. **H**ugh is **h**ighly skilled at **h**at tricks, while **H**arry can tell **h**ilarious jokes. Once during a show in **H**awaii, **H**arry **h**it **H**ugh on the fore**h**ead with a **h**ot dog. **H**ugh **h**id the **h**ot dog under his **h**at and danced the **h**ula. It was a **h**uge success!

Think about it

Think about the "r" in Portuguese. Is it always the same sound? What about in English? Is there any variant of the "r" in Portuguese that is similar to /r/ in English?

Pronounce these words slowly and pay attention to the way you articulate the /r/.

rose	a**rr**ive	ga**r**den	fou**r**
red	co**rr**ect	f**r**ee	ca**r**

Close up

The /r/ in English is pronounced like in some places in the countryside of São Paulo and Minas Gerais, for example. Say *porta aberta* very slowly like people from these places. Can you feel your tongue curving backwards? Now use the same sound to say *ar...* Keep the /r/ and say *ar...rose*, *ar...red*. That's the English /r/.

Zoom in

46 Exercise 1: Pronounce these words curving back your tongue:

dee**r** – ca**r**e – si**r** – fi**r**e
ca**r**d – hea**r**t – ce**r**tain
road – **r**eal – **r**epeat – **r**ed
b**r**own – g**r**een – f**r**ont – t**r**uck
p**r**actice – th**r**ee

47 Exercise 2: Repeat these sentences.

The **r**oad to **R**ome is dange**r**ous in the winte**r**.
Decembe**r**, Janua**r**y and Feb**r**ua**r**y a**r**e summe**r** months in the no**r**the**r**n hemisphe**r**e.
Ricky **R**ica**r**do was a cha**r**acte**r** in a popula**r** Ame**r**ican TV p**r**og**r**am.
__R__ock'n'__R__oll Pa__r__ty Queen is a song f**r**om *G__r__ease*.

48 The Silent Corner

Attention to the silent "w" in these words. The first sound you hear is /r/!

~~w~~rong – ~~w~~rite – ~~w~~rap – ~~w~~rist – ~~w~~rinkle

Repeat these sentences.

She ~~w~~rote that the ~~w~~rist watch was ~~w~~rong. Don't ~~w~~rap it.

In context

49 Exercise 1: Repeat linking the sounds:

four Indians	dear Alice	for us
her umbrella	car engine	fire escape
wore a suit	our insurance	your Andy

50 Exercise 2: Listen to this letter. Pay attention to the linking sounds!

Dear Alice,

Yesterday I had a very strange dream. I met four Indians who had a problem with their car engine. One of them was trying to climb a fire escape to get to a person's apartment and use the phone. Another was sticking her umbrella in the engine to start it. The third wore a red dress and the fourth asked me, "Could you call our insurance company for us?" It was so weird!

Your Andy

Read the letter in pairs, checking each other's pronunciation. Then close your books and ask each other questions about the letter. How much can you remember?

Fun time

51 Sing the song along with the recording. Turn it off and sing it as a round song: one person starts, and then the second person starts singing the first line when the first person starts the second line and so on.

Row, row, row your boat
Gently down the stream
Merrily, merrily, merrily, merrily
Life is but a dream

Zoom in

52 Repeat these pairs of words contrasting /h/ and /r/.

home	–	**R**ome	**h**ate	–	**r**ate
hose	–	**r**ose	**h**ead	–	**r**ed
hat	–	**r**at	**h**ear	–	**r**ear
hole	–	**r**ole	**h**eight	–	**r**ight
habit	–	**r**abbit	**h**ide	–	**r**ide
hair	–	**r**are	**h**ope	–	**r**ope

Work in pairs. Choose five of the words above and dictate them to a classmate. Pronounce the words carefully so your friend won't mix them up!

Stay tuned

53 Circle the word you hear.

A hound dog or a round dog?

1. Look! There's a *hat* / *rat* under the bed.
2. *Hide* / *Ride* the bicycle.
3. How do you know *your height* / *you're right*?
4. Can you smell that old *hose* / *rose*?
5. This is a *hound* / *round* dog.
6. That's an old *habit* / *rabbit*.
7. *Home* / *Rome* is the best place to be at night.
8. I prefer the *head* / *red* post.
9. Wow! This is really *hair* / *rare*.
10. He *hated* / *rated* his performance.

In context

54 Listen to these names of songs.

House of the Rising Sun (The Animals)
A Hard Rain's Gonna Fall (Bob Dylan)
The Road to Hell (Chris Rea)
Here Comes the Rain Again (Eurythmics)
The Real Holy Place (Boogie Down Productions)
Home of the Range (Disney)
Raise Your Hands (Bon Jovi)
Hurry Home (Jon Anderson)
Red Hill Mining Town (U2)
Ready to Go Home (10 CC)

Conversation

55 Listen to the conversation and then read it in pairs.

Harry: Hi, Ruth. I have to deliver a report at Mr. Ron Howard's house, and I don't know how to get there.
Ruth: Well, Harry, do you have the address?
Harry: Yes, it's at the corner of Hudson Road and Harris Road.
Ruth: Oh, I know the way. It's near Richards Hill. Turn right on Hippy Avenue, then right again after Richards Hill. Then take another right and you are there!
Harry: Thanks for the hot tip, Ruth.

Fun time

Get into two groups. Write ten words with initial /h/ or /r/. When the two groups are ready, one volunteer from one group should choose a number, and a member of the opposite group should tell him the word secretly. The person then has 30 seconds to mouth the word silently for his group to guess. If the group can't guess the word, the person then has ten seconds to mime the word. The group scores a point for each word guessed – and pronounced – correctly. Then it's the other group's turn. Have fun!

1. ______________________________
2. ______________________________
3. ______________________________
4. ______________________________
5. ______________________________
6. ______________________________
7. ______________________________
8. ______________________________
9. ______________________________
10. ______________________________

Unit 4 – Final /l/

Think about it

Does Portuguese have a final /l/? Do Brazilians in general pronounce it? What happens in English?

How do you pronounce these words?

we**ll**	tab**le**	co**l**d
rea**l**	simp**le**	fa**l**se

Did your tongue touch the area just behind your upper front teeth every time you pronounced /l/? Were your lips rounded?

Close up

Portuguese has a final ***letter*** "l," but most Brazilians pronounce the final "l" as an ***u*** sound. So we say **Braziu*, **futebóu*, etc. In English, however, the final /l/ ***is*** pronounced as /l/. Say "la-la-la." Observe that your tongue touches the area just behind your upper front teeth. Observe your lips. They are not supposed to be rounded when you produce a final /l/. If you round your lips, you're saying "u" instead.

Zoom in

56 Exercise 1: Repeat these words looking at your teacher's mouth or at yourself in the mirror. Be careful not to round your lips.

ki**ll** – ca**ll** – Brazi**l** – te**ll**
possib**le** – bicyc**le** – jung**le** – unc**le**
she**l**f – mi**l**k – twe**l**ve – o**l**d

57 Exercise 2: Repeat these phrases after the model.

a**ll** possib**le**
in a **l**itt**le** whi**le**
who**le** artic**le**
sma**ll** bicyc**le**
he**l**p o**l**d peop**le**
fi**ll** the bott**le**
in the midd**le** of the tab**le**
doub**le** troub**le**
ki**ll** a bu**ll**

Now read the phrases in pairs, observing each other's mouths. Can you make sentences with the words and phrases above?

58 The Silent Corner

The "l" is silent in these words. Listen and repeat:

ha~~l~~f – ca~~l~~f   ta~~l~~k – wa~~l~~k – cha~~l~~k   wou~~l~~d – shou~~l~~d – cou~~l~~d
ba~~l~~m – pa~~l~~m – ca~~l~~m   sa~~l~~mon – Linco~~l~~n

Get your tongue around it

59 Exercise 1: Notice how we abbreviate the future tense. Listen:

I'**ll**	we'**ll**
he'**ll**	you'**ll**
she'**ll**	they'**ll**

60 Exercise 2: Listen to the words and put them in the correct place in the sentence. Remember to link the sounds. Follow the example.

I'**ll** eat it.
Model: *he*
You: *He'**ll** eat it.*
Model: *adore*
You: *He'**ll** adore it.*

Do it mentally (in silence) first. Then play the track again and do it orally.

In context

61 Exercise 1: Repeat linking the sounds:

Attention! This is what you really say.
Brazil is = Bra-zi-liz / people are = peo-pa-lar

Brazi**l** is	peop**le** are	carefu**l** about	beautifu**l** attractions
trave**l** on	wi**ll** enjoy	wi**ll** always	amp**le** environment

62 Exercise 2: Now listen to this paragraph.

Brazi**l** is a wonderfu**l** country for peop**le** to visit. Peop**le** are a**l**ways carefu**l** about choosing a trave**l** destination, but if you trave**l** on vacation or business, Brazi**l** is the place for you. You wi**ll** enjoy the beautifu**l** attractions Brazi**l** offers! You wi**ll** a**l**ways remember our amp**le** environment and our beautifu**l** beaches, our wi**l**dlife and our friendly peop**le**. Come to Brazi**l**!

Read the paragraph in pairs, observing each other's mouths.

Conversation

63 Jill and Randall want to go to the mall. Listen to their conversation.

Ji**ll**: Randa**ll**, I fee**l** like going to the ma**ll**. I want to get a beautifu**l** jewe**l** for Gai**l**. She turns twe**l**ve next Apri**l**. Can I borrow your whee**l**s?

Randa**ll**: My whee**l**s, Ji**ll**? My car is an origina**l** Beet**le**. I'**ll** drive you if you like.

Ji**ll**: Wonderfu**l**! Is it possib**le** you'**ll** go shopping with me as we**ll**? I need your he**l**p to choose the most beautifu**l**, incredib**le**, and delightfu**l** jewe**l** I can find.

Randa**ll**: You'**ll** do a**ll** this for Gai**l**? Wow, she's a he**ll** of a lucky pood**le**.

Now read the conversation in pairs.

Stay tuned

64 Exercise 1: Can you hear the difference the /l/ makes? Listen to these pairs of words.

so – sou**l**
bow – bow**l**
go – goa**l**
sewed – so**l**d
road – ro**ll**ed

65 Exercise 2: Now listen and repeat:

sow/sew/so	–	soul/sole	sewed	–	sold
bow	–	bowl	rode/road	–	rolled
go	–	goal	code	–	cold
mow	–	mole	ode	–	old
row	–	role/roll	coat	–	colt

66 Exercise 3: Listen to the recording and circle the words you hear.

1. The woman *sewed* / *sold* the old clothes.
2. John put the *bow* / *bowl* on the table.
3. He shouted, "*Go*" / "*Goal*!"
4. I like the *coat* / *colt*.
5. Get the first *row* / *role*.
6. Do you have a *code* / *cold*?

Work in pairs. Student A reads out a sentence choosing one of the words, and Student B has to identify which word was used (first or second option).

Zoom in

67 Exercise 1: When /l/ and /r/ come after some vowels, we can sometimes hear a schwa sound /ə/ before /l/ and /r/. Listen to these examples:

feel – loyal – file – pool
fear – cure – player

68 Exercise 2: Now listen and repeat.

feel	fear
jewel	cure
loyal	fire
file	player
school	weird
child	here
tail/tale	tired

69 Exercise 3: Repeat these sentences.

The loyal players are tired.
The files were destroyed by the fire.
I fear school fires.
That weird child doesn't go to school.
You'll feel better after you're cured.
The child enjoys the tale about the jewels.

70 When /l/ is in an unstressed syllable after /t/ or /d/, no vowel sound is pronounced by most native speakers, even if a vowel letter appears in the written form. This sound is called **syllabic l** and it's represented as /l̩/ Listen:

hospital – middle – bottle – candle – total – needle

/fə'nætɪk fər fə'nɛtɪks/

Match the transcriptions and the definitions.

1.	/sku:l/	a.	___ the place where you go when you're sick
2.	/'dʒu:əl/	b.	___ complete
3.	/tʃaɪld/	c.	___ you use it to sew
4.	/'lɔɪəl/	d.	___ not big
5.	/smɔl/	e.	___ a precious stone
6.	/'ni:dl̩/	f.	___ a place where you study
7.	/'hɑspɪtl̩/	g.	___ not an adult
8.	/hoʊl/	h.	___ used to describe a dog

Fun time

✎ Do you know this famous Abraham Lincoln quote? In pairs, fill in the blanks with the words in the box. The first pair to complete the quote correctly gets ten points. Each word pronounced correctly is worth two points. Good luck!

fool – people – all

"You can ______________ ______________ the ______________ some of the time, and some of the ______________ ______________ the time, but you cannot ______________ ______________ the ______________ ______________ of the time."

Unit 5 - STOPS: /p/ /t/ /k/ /b/ /d/ /g/

Peter Piper picked a peck of pickled peppers.

Think about it

✎ Mark true or false:

1. The Portuguese word *pai* and the English word *pie* sound the same. ___
2. The only difference between /t/ and /d/ is that /t/ is voiceless and /d/ is voiced. ___
3. The sounds /p/, /t/ and /k/ have something in common besides being voiceless stops. ___
4. Regardless of the position in the word, /k/ in English always sounds the same. ___

Don't look at the **Answer Key** yet. Study the unit to the end and then check your answers.

Close up

Aspiration is the extra puff of air that is released with some sounds. Voiceless stops (/p/, /t/ and /k/) are aspirated when they appear in ***initial*** or in ***stressed*** position. So, the only difference between the Portuguese word *pai* and the English word *pie* is that the /p/ in the English word is aspirated.

71 Exercise 1: Listen to the difference.

Portuguese	English
pai	pie

72 Exercise 2: Now contrast.

Kate – gate   time – dime   pill – bill

The aspiration is the main difference between the voiceless sounds and their voiced counterparts (/b/, /d/ and /g/). If you don't aspirate the /p/ in *pill*, a native speaker might understand *bill* instead. Native speakers ***expect*** these voiceless stops to be aspirated, and if they don't hear the puff of air, they assume the voiced counterparts are being produced instead.

Get a piece of paper. Let the top part touch your nose while you hold the page halfway through in front of your mouth. Say the word *pai* a few times. The paper shouldn't move. Then say the word *pie* aspirating the /p/. If you aspirate correctly, the piece of paper should move visibly.

Zoom in

73 Exercise 1: Repeat these words with /p/, /t/ and /k/ in **initial position**. Make sure you aspirate them.

pen – **t**ea – **c**at
price – **t**rue – **c**ry
play – **t**win – **c**lose

74 Exercise 2: Repeat these words aspirating /p/, /t/ and /k/ in **stressed position**.

re**p**ort – ob**t**ain – be**c**ome
a**pp**roach – a**tt**ack – a**cc**ount

75 Listen to the difference in aspiration in the following words:

noun	**verb**
récord	recórd
éxport	expórt
díscount	discóunt
ímpact	impáct

76 Exercise 3: When the voiceless stops are in **initial position** but are **not stressed**, the aspiration is **weaker**. Listen and repeat.

posítion – **c**orréct – **t**errífic
políce – **c**ondúctor – **t**ogéther

77 Exercise 4: Repeat these sentences, aspirating /p/, /t/ and /k/ **in initial or stressed position**.

The **c**ook is **p**utting a **p**ie on the **k**itchen **t**able.
Tim **c**an't **t**urn on his com**p**uter on **T**uesday.
Tell **K**ate the **p**rice of the **t**rain and **p**lane **t**ickets.
Pat **t**ried to **c**ome to **T**exas by **c**able **c**ar.

78 Exercise 5: /p/, /t/ and /k/ preceded by /s/ are not aspirated. Repeat this sentence.

The **Sp**anish **sp**y **sc**reamed at the **sk**inny **st**udent.

79 Exercise 6: /b/, /d/ and /g/ are never aspirated. Repeat these words after the model.

boy – **d**oll – **g**uy
em**b**race – a**d**ore – a**g**ain
bring – **d**rink – **g**reen
black – **d**warf – **g**lad

80 The Silent Corner

Exercise 1: The "p" is silent in these words. Listen and repeat:

~~p~~neumonia – ~~p~~sychology – ~~p~~sychiatrist – cu~~p~~board
recei~~p~~t – ras~~p~~berry

Exercise 2: The "t" is silent is these words. Listen and repeat:

lis~~t~~en – fas~~t~~en – Chris~~t~~mas – mor~~t~~gage – cas~~t~~le – whis~~t~~le

Exercise 3: The "k" is silent in these words. Listen and repeat:

~~k~~night – ~~k~~nife – ~~k~~nee – ~~k~~now – ~~k~~nock – ~~k~~nack – ~~k~~nit – ~~k~~nob

Exercise 4: The "b" is silent in these words. Listen and repeat:

dum~~b~~ – thum~~b~~ – plum~~b~~er – clim~~b~~ – clim~~b~~er – bom~~b~~ – lam~~b~~
tom~~b~~ – de~~b~~t

Exercise 5: The "d" is silent is these words. Listen and repeat:

We~~d~~nesday – han~~d~~kerchief – han~~d~~bag – han~~d~~some – han~~d~~made

Exercise 6: The "g" is silent in these words. Listen and repeat:

si~~g~~n – resi~~g~~n – assi~~g~~n – desi~~g~~n – rei~~g~~n – campai~~g~~n
~~g~~nome – ~~g~~nu – ~~g~~nat – ~~g~~naw

Get your tongue around it

81 Exercise 1: Be careful not to add a vowel sound when the stops appear in final position. Listen.

He's a co**p**.
She's eigh**t**.
I'm si**ck**.

This is Bo**b**.
He's ma**d**.
Play ta**g**.

Exercise 2: In groups of three, pretend you're introducing some friends. Be careful not to add a vowel sound at the end. Follow the example:

A: Bob, this is Jake. Jake, this is Bob.
B: Nice to meet you, Jake.
C: Nice to meet you, Bob.

Pat – Mike – Fred – Janet – Kate – Margaret – Peg Violet – Alfred – Clark – David – Jack – Rob

Conversation

82 Listen to this conversation. All the stops are in bold. Underline the ones that are aspirated.

Kate: Hi, **T**ed. **T**om jus**t** **c**alle**d** as**k**ing if you **c**oul**d** len**d** him your vi**d**eo **c**amera.

Ted: Than**k**s for **t**elling me, **K**a**t**e. I**t**'s abou**t** **t**ime **T**om bough**t** his own e**q**ui**p**ment, **d**on'**t** you thin**k**? I**t**'s the **t**enth **t**ime he's as**ked** to borrow mine!

Kate: Be **p**a**t**ien**t**, **T**e**d**. Af**t**er all, **T**om jus**t** wan**t**s **t**o shoo**t** his **c**ousin's birth**d**ay **p**ar**t**y.

Ted: O**K**. When's the o**cc**asion?

Kate: O**ct**o**b**er four**t**eenth.

Ted: So **T**om's **g**oing **t**o **b**e the cinema**t**ographer a**t** my **g**e**t**-**t**o**g**ether? So wha**t** are we waiting for? **T**om nee**d**s tha**t** **c**am**c**order righ**t** away!

Read the conversation in pairs, making sure to aspirate /p/, /t/ and /k/ in initial and stressed position.

Zoom in

Exercise 1: Sometimes students confuse the aspirated /t/ with /tʃ/. Compare these words.

initial /t/ x /tʃ/			final /t/ x /tʃ/		
two	–	chew	art	–	arch
tease	–	cheese	beet/beat	–	beach
tip	–	chip	cat	–	catch
tin	–	chin	eat	–	each
tear	–	cheer	Pete	–	peach
tea	–	chi	bent	–	bench

83 Now listen and repeat.

84 Exercise 2: Repeat these words. Pay attention not to say /tʃ/ instead of /t/.

tea – **t**eacher – **t**each – **t**eam – **t**eens – **t**eeth – **T**-shirt

85 Exercise 3: Repeat these sentences.

The **t**eenagers **t**eased the **t**eacher.
Tha**t** ca**t** ea**t**s bee**t**.
Tim wan**t**s **t**wo **T**-shir**t**s.
Pe**te** drank **t**ea with his **t**eacher.

Stay tuned

86 Check the pictures according to the words you hear.

Go back and write the corresponding words. Then work in pairs. Say one word and your friend will point to the right picture.

Zoom in

87 Exercise 1: Compare these words:

/d/	–	/dʒ/
D	–	G
dean	–	Jean
dear	–	jeer
deep	–	jeep
dig	–	jig
dim	–	gym

/d/	–	/dʒ/
aid	–	age
bad	–	badge

88 Exercise 2: Repeat these sentences.

Dog is spelled D-O-G.
Dean Jean Leed opened the new gym.
The Red Badge of Courage is a book about the dim war days.
The aid tried hard to conceal her age.

Stay tuned

89 Listen and repeat the sentences, circling the word you hear.

1. *Dean* / *Jean* Smith is my friend.
2. My name starts with a *D* / *G*.
3. Is there a way we can *aid* / *age* him?
4. We are going to *dig* / *jig*.
5. Look at that nice *beet* / *beach*.
6. That was a bad *cat* / *catch*.

Think about it

Have you ever noticed that /t/ and /d/ sometimes sound like the Portuguese "r" as in *arara*? In what position do they sound like that?

Which of these pronunciations of the word potato do you think are possible?

a. /pəˈteɪtoʊ/
b. /pəˈteɪɾoʊ/
c. /pəˈɾeɪɾoʊ/

Close up

In American English, /t/ and /d/ **in unstressed position** become a flap [ɾ] in these situations:

between vowels within words: better, meadow
between vowels in connected speech: get up, hide out
between /r/ and a vowel sound within words: party, birdie, forty
between /r/ and a vowel sound in connected speech: part of the problem, art and history
between a vowel and a syllabic /l/: little, beetle

Considering the explanation above, the word *potato* can be pronounced /pəˈteɪtoʊ/ or /pəˈteɪɾoʊ/, but never */pəˈɾeɪɾoʊ/, because the first /t/ is stressed.

You don't have to produce a flap [ɾ], but it's important to be able to recognize it once it's produced by most speakers of American English.

Zoom in

90 Exercise 1: Repeat these words:

la**d**y – me**t**al – star**t**ed – pre**tt**y – da**t**ed – compu**t**er – we**dd**ing

91 Exercise 2: Repeat these phrases:

a lo**t** of me**t**al	pu**t** up with the la**d**y	hi**t** i**t** again
a**t** eigh**t** o'clock	nee**d**e**d** it	ha**t**e**d** us

92 When a "t" comes after an "n" in unstressed position, it can be omitted. Compare these two correct pronunciations:
printer – center – twenty – seventy
So, winter = winner!

93 Exercise 3: Repeat these sentences.

The pre**tt**y la**d**y go**t** a lo**t** of we**dd**ing gifts.
Tha**t** old compu**t**er is da**t**ed.
The par**t**y ha**d** alrea**d**y star**t**ed when Pa**t** entered.

94 Exercise 4: When we use a flap, words with "t" or "d" end up sounding the same. Compare:

waiter	=	wader	matter	=	madder
otter	=	odder	hearty	=	hardy
latter	=	ladder	parity	=	parody

In context

95 Exercise 1: Repeat linking the sounds.

reward allowed	opened it	found a
job at	check-out	bag of
Jack and	like a	Bob agreed
Bob almost	spend it	Jack insisted

96 Exercise 2: Fill in the blanks with the phrases above.

________________ Bob are brothers. They would ________________ new car, so they got a job at a supermarket. Jack is a cashier at the ____________ counter, and Bob is an attendant at Customer Service. One day, Jack found a ________________ groceries under the counter. Jack ________________, and ________________ lot of money inside. ________________ couldn't believe his eyes, and wanted to _______________ all right away. ___________ that they return the bag to the police. _______________ and they did it. They were very happy to hear there was a reward. The _______________ them to get their car and quit the _______________ the supermarket.

Now listen and check.

/fəˈnætɪk fər fəˈnɛtɪks/

Decipher the message.

/ðə ˈæŋgri kɪŋ prəˈkleɪmd ðət ðə prɪnˈsɛs ˈkʊdnt baɪ ə pɛt ˈpɔrkyəˌpaɪn/

____

____

Fun time

On the first page of this unit you read the beginning of a nursery rhyme. The complete version goes:

Peter Piper picked a peck of pickled peppers
If Peter Piper picked a peck of pickled peppers
How many peppers did Peter Piper pick?

In small groups, write similar rhymes with the /k/ or the /t/ sounds. Read your rhymes to the class, remembering to aspirate the voiceless stops in ***initial*** or ***stressed*** position. Hold a competition: the funniest rhyme wins!

Wrap up

Go back to **Think about it** and go over the questions again. Then check your answers in the **Answer Key**.

Unit 6 - /ʃ/ and /ʒ/, /tʃ/ and /dʒ/, /f/ and /v/

Think about it

1. The sound /ʃ/ is spelled…

a. sh
b. s
c. ss
d. ch
e. ti
f. ci
g. all of the above

2. The sound /tʃ/ is spelled…

a. sh
b. s
c. ss
d. ch
e. ti
f. ci
g. all of the above

Can you find examples to justify your answers?

Don't look at the **Answer Key** yet. Study the unit to the end and then check your answers.

Close up

The sound /ʃ/ is usually spelled "sh" as in ***she***, but it can be spelled "s" as in *sugar*, "ss" as in *issue*, "ci" as in *social* or "ti" as in *action*. The sound /tʃ/ is usually spelled "ch" as in ***church***, but it can also be spelled "tu" as in *picture*.

Zoom in

98 Exercise 1: Listen to these words with /ʃ/:

shop – **sh**ut – fi**sh** – ru**sh**
i**ss**ue – pre**ss**ure – in**s**ure – **s**ure
spe**ci**al – o**ce**an – effi**ci**ent – so**ci**al
na**ti**on – essen**ti**al – ini**ti**al

99 Exercise 2: Some foreign words where "ch" is pronounced /ʃ/ are:

ma**ch**ine – **ch**ef – **Ch**icago – musta**ch**e – para**ch**ute
champagne – Mi**ch**igan

100 Exercise 3: Repeat these sentences.

She wi**sh**es to ca**sh** her in**s**urance money unsuspi**ci**ously.
Take a **sh**ower, wa**sh** your hair and **sh**ave before you meet **Sh**eila.
Sugar is tra**sh**, but my ma**ch**ine **s**urely needs it.
The **ch**ef a**ss**ured **S**ean he had **ch**ampagne on his musta**ch**e.

101 Exercise 4: Now listen to these words with the /tʃ/ sound:

church – **ch**ild – **ch**at
pay**ch**eck – ba**ch**elor – en**ch**antment
fu**tu**re – si**tu**ation – na**tu**ral – furni**tu**re

102 Exercise 5: Repeat these sentences:

Chuck **ch**atted with **Ch**arlie.
They want to wa**tch** the ma**tch**.
Fe**tch** the new ba**tch** of **ch**ili beans in the ki**tch**en.
Can you pic**tu**re the si**tu**ation?

103 "Ch" can be pronounced /k/. Listen to these words:
Christmas – **ch**orus – e**ch**o – psy**ch**iatrist – me**ch**anic
heada**che** – **ch**emical – ar**ch**itecture

Stay tuned

104 Exercise 1: Repeat these pairs of words:

/ʃ/ – /tʃ/	/ʃ/ – /tʃ/
share – chair	wash – watch
sherry – cherry	cash – catch
shoe – chew	wish – which/witch
shore – chore	bush – butch
shin – chin	mush – much
ship – chip	
shop – chop	
sheep – cheap	

105 Exercise 2: Listen and check the correct picture.

1. a ______________________

1. b ______________________

2. a ____________________

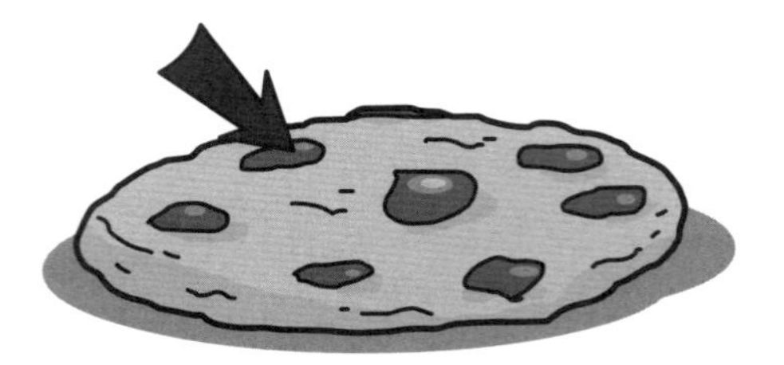

2. b ____________________

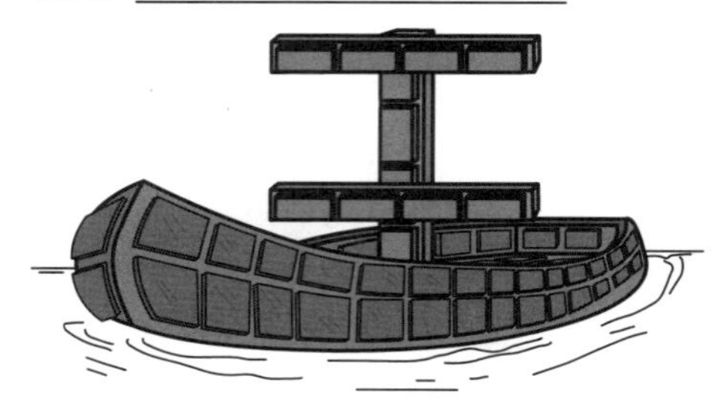

3. a ____________________

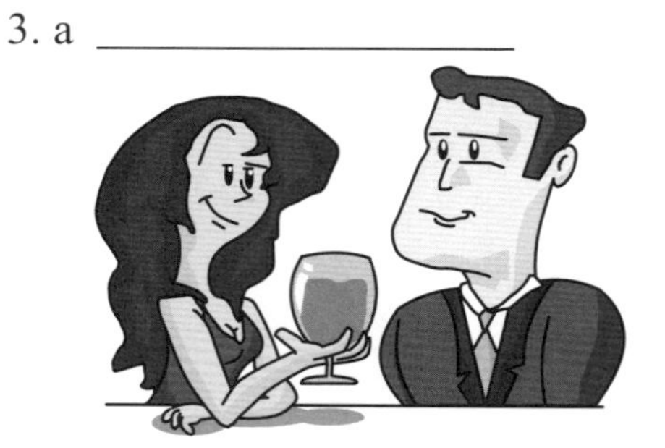

3. b ____________________

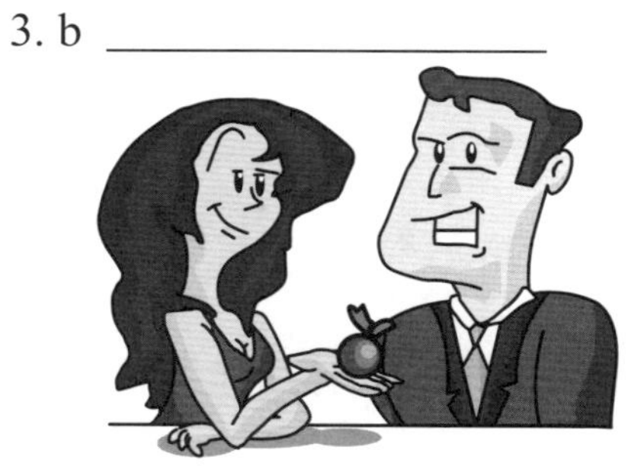

4. a ____________________

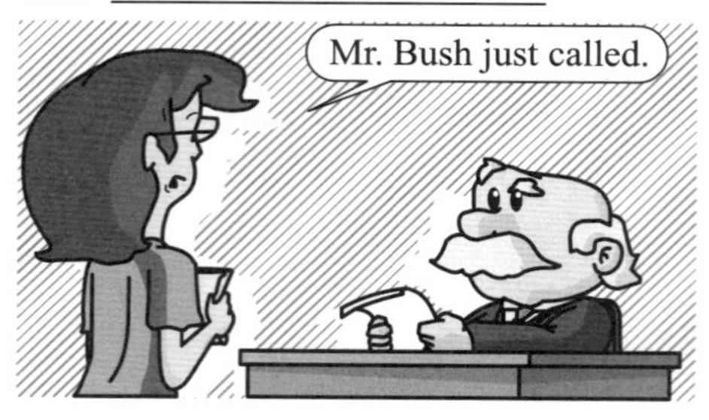
Mr. Bush just called.

4. b ____________________

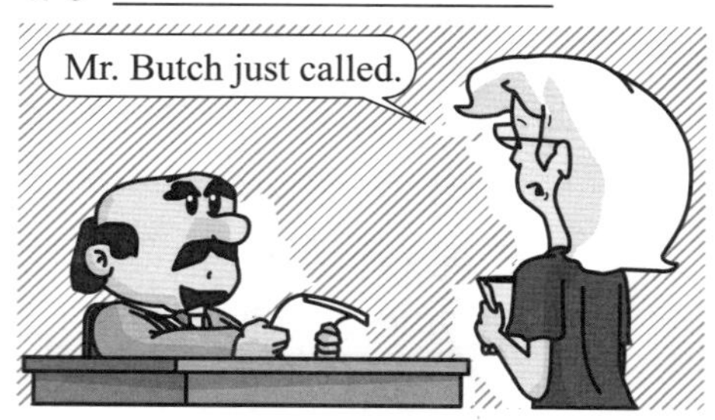
Mr. Butch just called.

5. a ____________________

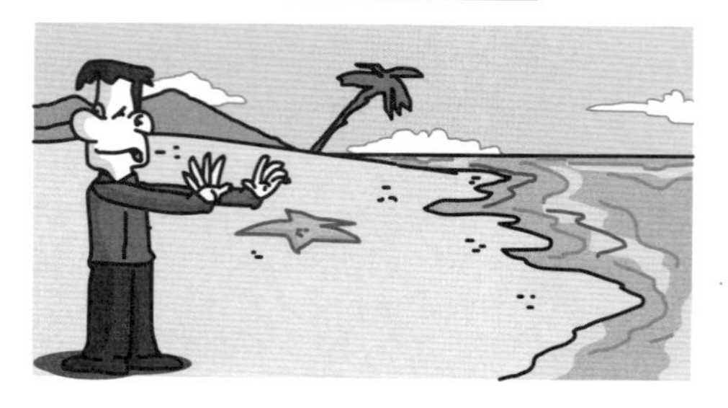

5. b ____________________

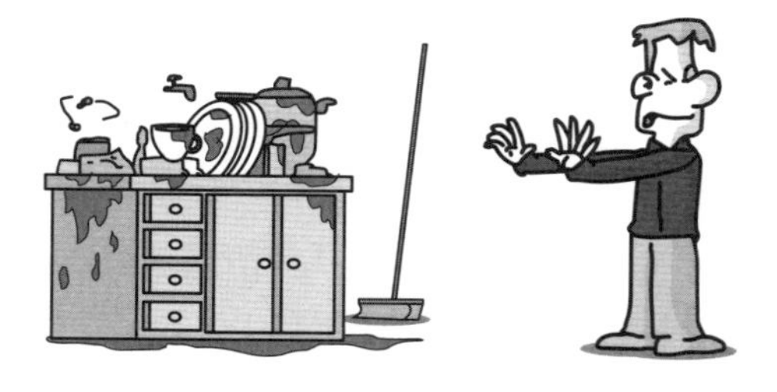

Listen again and write down the sentences you hear. Then write the corresponding pair.

Get your tongue around it

106 Exercise 1: Repeat these phrases, linking the sounds:

push up
fish and chips
cash advance
which employee
inch on
much enjoyment

107 Exercise 2: Now substitute the verbs as in the example, paying attention to the final /ʃ/ or /tʃ/. Remember to **stress the verbs**.

Model: Wash your hair!
You: I'll wash it!
Model: Fetch the book.
You: I'll fetch it!

Cash the check.
Catch the bus.
Coach the dog.
Push the car.

Exercise 3: Now work in pairs. Come up with more sentences like these. You can use these verbs:

watch – mash – brush – scratch – wish – fish – etc

In context

108 Listen to the paragraph and fill in the blanks with the missing words.

Mitch and Sean share a ________________ shack by the ________________. Mitch usually ________________ a coach to the ________________ to go ________________ on weekends. Sean, on the other hand, ________________ prefers to drive his Chevy down to the shore in ________________, when there aren't kids ________________ all around, so he can sit on a bench and ________________ the sea in peace. Mitch and Sean never go to the __________ together, and they think their arrangement is perfect!

Now listen again and read the paragraph along with the model.

You are a mira**ge**! Can I massa**ge** your feet, my Pari**s**ian trea**s**ure?

Think about it

✎ True or false?

1. The sound /ʒ/ is a frequent sound in English. ___
2. The sound /ʒ/ occurs in initial, medial and final position. ___
3. The sound /ʒ/ is usually spelled with "s" between vowels. ___
4. The sound /dʒ/ occurs in initial, medial and final position. ___
5. The sound /dʒ/ is usually spelled "j" or "g." ___

Don't look at the **Answer Key** yet. Study the unit to the end and then check your answers.

Close up

The sound /ʒ/ is not very common in English, occurring mostly in medial position. It's usually spelled with "s" between vowels (*pleasure, usual*). It also occurs in final position in French words (*mirage, espionage*). It doesn't occur in initial position, except in the French word *genre*.

The sound /dʒ/ is a lot more common, and it occurs in all positions. It's usually spelled "j" as in *just* or "gi" or "ge" as in *giant* or *general*. It's also spelled "du" as in *gradual*.

Zoom in

109 Exercise 1: Listen to these words with /ʒ/.

A**s**ia – ca**s**ual – u**s**ually
lei**s**ure – trea**s**ure – mea**s**ure – clo**s**ure
illu**s**ion – confu**s**ion – televi**s**ion
bei**ge** – massa**ge** – corsa**ge**

The word ***garage*** can be pronounced in three different ways:
Am. E. /gəˈrɑʒ/ or /gəˈrɑdʒ/
Br. E. /ˈgærədʒ/

110 Exercise 2: Repeat these sentences with /ʒ/.

I met an A**s**ian man and a Pari**s**ian girl on my trip to Indone**s**ia.
Bert u**s**ually tests his vi**s**ion.
Nancy trea**s**ures the moments of plea**s**ure she gets when Tony massa**ge**s her feet.

111 Exercise 3: Now listen to these words with /dʒ/.

just – **j**oke – **G**ermany – **g**enerous
jet – a**dj**ust – en**g**ineer
bri**dge** – colle**ge** – sta**ge**
gra**du**ate – e**du**cate – gra**du**al – indivi**du**al

112 Exercise 4: Repeat these sentences with /dʒ/.

John **j**otted down some **j**oyful words in his **J**apanese notebook.
Jim's **g**eneration never wore **j**eans.
Jeff en**j**oys oran**ge** **j**uice and **j**am.
E**du**cation is important to the gra**du**ate student.

Get your tongue around it

113 Listen to the words and put them in the correct place in the sentence. Follow the example.

Model: *John is an Asian engineer.*
You: *John is an Asian engineer.* (repetition)
Model: *Japanese*
You: *John is a Japanese engineer.*
Model: *John is a Japanese engineer. Educator*
You: *John is a Japanese educator.*

generous – casual – jazz musician – knowledgeable – treasured – judge

Do it mentally (in silence) first. Then play the track again and do it orally.

Conversation

114 Exercise 1: Listen to this conversation.

Gina: Pic**tu**re this, **Sh**eila! **S**ean had the coura**ge** to ask me casually if I wi**sh**ed to pur**ch**ase something I trea**s**ure as a birthday present. He said he wouldn't have a **ch**ance to go out and sear**ch** for something spe**c**ial.

Sheila: Oh, **G**ina. That's na**tu**ral: men are clueless. I'm **s**ure he means well. He **j**ust doesn't want to get you something that you'll have to ex**ch**ange later, as it u**s**ually happens. As a puni**sh**ment, you **sh**ould get yourself something horribly po**sh**, as Pari**s**ian perfume or a **J**apanese wat**ch**.

✎ Exercise 2: Write the words in bold above next to the corresponding symbols.

1. /ʃ/ ______________________________
2. /tʃ/______________________________
3. /ʒ/ ______________________________
4. /dʒ/ - *just*, _________________________

Zoom in

115 In English, the sounds /t/ and /d/ can change to /tʃ/ and /dʒ/ when a word ends in /t/ and /d/ and is followed by /y/:

what you do
that you can
at your time
about you

need you
would you do
bide your time
guide you

Sometimes, however, some speakers prefer to pronounce these junctures with a glottal stop [ʔ], which is a sound formed by stopping the air stream at the vocal folds. Listen again and compare the way the phrases were recorded before and now.

Think about it

✎ Do these tasks in small groups.

1. Write words with these spellings for the /f/ sound:

f: ______________________________

ff: ______________________________

fe: ______________________________

ph: ______________________________

gh: ______________________________

2. Circle the last sound in the word ***have*** in these sentences:

a. I ha***ve*** a car: /f/ /v/
b. I ha***ve*** to go: /f/ /v/

3. The words *of* and *off*

a. sound exactly the same.
b. have the same vowel sound.
c. have the same consonant sound.
d. sound completely different.

4. The words *have* and *of* can sound the same. T F

Close up

Like the previous sounds /ʃ/, /tʃ/, /ʒ/ and /dʒ/, the sounds /f/ and /v/ don't represent a challenge for Brazilians in terms of articulation. Just make sure never to add a vowel after these sounds when they appear in final position, like in *arrive* /ə'raɪv/ and *wife* /waɪf/.

Zoom in

116 Exercise 1: Repeat these words with final /f/ and /v/. Don't add a vowel sound at the end.

i**f** – o**ff** – wi**fe**
lau**gh** – enou**gh** – cou**gh** – **ph**otogra**ph**
arri**ve** – li**ve** – mo**ve** – ca**ve**

117 Compare:

1 syllable	**2 syllables**
cough	coffee
stuff	stuffy
move	movie
wave	wavy
have	heavy
/hæv/	/'hɛvi/

118 Exercise 2: Contrast *of* and *off*:

I want a bowl *of* ice cream.
He needs a carton *of* eggs.
} Before vowels: /əv/

I drank a cup *of* tea.
Give me a glass *of* milk.
Would you like a cup *of* coffee?
} Before consonants: /ə/

Please turn *off* the TV.
Take *off* your shoes. } Always /ɔf/

119 Exercise 3: Observe how *have* is pronounced:

I have a book. (/hæv/)
I have to go. (/hæf/)
I should have gone. (/əv/, the same as *of*)

In context

Practice these phrases.

if I /ɪf‿aɪ/
if it /ɪf‿ɪt/
life again /laɪf‿əˈgɛn/

120 Listen to these quotes.

If *I had to li**ve** my li**fe** again, I'd make the same mistakes, only sooner.* Tallulah Bankhead (1903 – 1968)

*My mother lo**v**ed children — she would ha**ve** gi**v**en anything **if** I had been one.* Groucho Marx (1890 – 1977)

If *I knew I was going to li**ve** this long, I'd ha**ve** taken better care of mysel**f**.* Mickey Mantle (1931 – 1995)

*The go**v**ernment's **v**iew o**f** the economy could be summed up in a **f**ew short **ph**rases: **If** it mo**ve**s, tax it. **If** it keeps mo**v**ing, regulate it. And **if** it stops mo**v**ing, subsidize it.* Ronald Reagan (1911 – 2004)

/fəˈnætɪk fər fəˈnɛtɪks/

✎ Write the phonetic symbols for the underlined letters.

which	judge	situation
/tʃ/	___ ___	___ ___
changing	education	physician
___ ___	___ ___	___ ___
tough	Indonesian	childish
___	___	___ ___

Fun time

How many of these words can you include in just one sentence? Have a competition in your class. The group that includes the most words in a **meaningful** way gets five points. Each word that is pronounced correctly is worth one point. The group with the highest score is the winner! You have three minutes!

huge – camouflage – chat – collision – cough – flashlight – French
jump – jury – leave – love – measure – peach – rough – save
shower – stuff – trash

Wrap up

Go back to **Think about it** and go over the questions again. Then check your answers in the **Answer Key**.

Unit 7 - /s/ and /z/

Think about it

Read these statements, analyze your speech and write true or false. Correct the false statements.

1. There are three syllables in the word *smile*. ___
2. The last sound in the words *bus*, *house* and *base* is /s/. ___
3. *This* and *these* end in the same sound. ___
4. The verb to *use* and the noun *use* are not pronounced the same way. ___
5. When I say *Yes, it is*, what we hear is /yɛzɪtɪz/. ___
6. Both "ss" in the word *possessive* have the same sound. ___

Don't look at the **Answer Key** now! Study the unit to the end and then check your answers.

Close up

In Portuguese, final "–s" is pronounced /z/ when followed by a voiced sound. Compare: *mas* (/z/) *eu*, *mas* (/s/) *tu*. The same happens with "s" between vowels: *casa* /z/. For this reason, students tend to mispronounce common words such as *basic* /ˈbeɪsɪk/ and *fantasy* /ˈfæntəsi/. In English, however, a written "s" can be pronounced /s/ or /z/, and that does NOT change depending on the environment. For example, if the final sound is /s/, it will always be /s/, regardless of the following sound. Observe:

less /lɛs/ **c**omplicated
less /lɛs/ **i**mportant

Zoom in

121 Exercise 1: These words end in /s/.

ye**s** – thi**s**– cla**ss** – bu**s** – addre**ss**
hou**se** – mou**se** – blou**se**
increa**se** – decrea**se** – ba**se** – ca**se**

Note the pronunciation of the word *address*:
noun: /əˈdrɛs/ or /ˈædrɛs/
verb: /əˈdrɛs/

122 Exercise 2: These words are also pronounced with /s/.

ba**s**ic – ba**s**is – u**se**ful – u**se**less – fanta**s**y

123 Exercise 3: Pay attention to the pronunciation of the suffix *–ous*. It's pronounced /əs/ as in *bus*.

fam**ous** – gener**ous** – glori**ous** – courage**ous** – vari**ous**

Close up

Initial /s/ followed by a consonant also poses a problem for Brazilian speakers. As we don't have this combination, students tend to insert a vowel sound before the /s/, adding an extra syllable to the word.

Zoom in

124 Exercise 1: Let's practice the initial /s/. Say sssss. Now do the same as on the recording.

ssssstay – sssspeak – sssssmart

125 Exercise 2: Repeat these words starting with /s/. They are all **one-syllable words**, so don't add an extra vowel at the beginning.

smile – **s**chool – **s**peak – **s**tage
sleep – **s**cale – **s**neeze
scratch – **s**prain – **s**traight

126 Exercise 3: The prefixes *dis-* and *mis-* are also pronounced with /s/. Repeat:

disappointed – **dis**order – **dis**appear – **dis**organized – **dis**honest
misunderstand – **mis**use – **mis**inform – **mis**interpret

> Attention: *Disaster* and *disease* are pronounced with /z/ because *dis* is not a prefix in these words!

127 Exercise 4: Repeat these sentences.

Ye**s**, you mi**s**understood me. Thi**s** gue**s**t is famou**s**, but he won't re**c**eive **s**pecial treatment.
I di**s**agree on going to her hou**se** by bu**s**.
The mou**se** ran down **S**tuart'**s** **s**tudent'**s** blou**se**.

Get your tongue around it

128 Exercise 1: Listen to the words and put them in the correct place in the sentence. Remember to link the sounds. Follow the example.

Pay attention how this is pronounced:
The house is special = The hou sis pecial.
/sɪs/
The second /s/ is a little longer.

The house is spacious.
Model: Bus.
You: The bus is spacious.
Model: The bus is spacious. Special
You: The bus is special.

Do it mentally (in silence) first. Then play the track again and do it orally.

129 Exercise 2: Remember that *yes* has a final /s/. So listen to these oral cues and answer positively, like this: *Yes, I do.*
/saɪ/

Example:
Model: Are you Brazilian?
You: Yes, I am.

Now you do it.

Conversation

130 This is the first class in the Basic 1 course. Miss Smith is the teacher. Listen to the conversation.

Steve: Miss **S**mith?
Miss Smith: Come in, come in. What'**s** your name?
Steve: **S**teve Gar**c**ia, but...
Miss Smith: Gar**c**ia? Are you **S**panish?
Steve: Well, my parents are from **S**pain, but...
Miss Smith: Is this a **s**kirt, Mr. Gar**c**ia?
Steve: Ye**s**, it is, Mi**ss**, but...
Miss Smith: Ju**s**t an**s**wer the que**s**tion! Is thi**s** a **s**carf?
Steve: Ye**s**, it is. I'm **s**orry, Mi**ss** **S**mith. I'm not a **s**tudent.
Miss Smith: You're not? That'**s** **s**trange! Why are you in this cla**ss**room?
Steve: Well, I'm a teacher, and thi**s** is my cla**ss**. Your cla**ss** is next door.

In pairs, role-play the conversation above substituting the words. You can choose among these:

bus – spaceship – school – skateboard – sled – slide – passport – snake

131 The Silent Corner

The "s" is not pronounced in these words:

ai~~s~~le /aɪl/ – i~~s~~land /ˈaɪlənd/
Arkansa~~s~~ /ˈɑrkənˌsɔ/ – Illinoi~~s~~ /ɪlɪˈnɔɪ/

Zoom in

132 Exercise 1: Repeat these words with the /z/ sound.

hi**s** – her**s** – their**s**
doe**s** – wa**s** – say**s** – i**s**
re**s**ort – bu**s**iness – ea**s**y
who**s**e – prai**s**e – becau**s**e

Exercise 2: Match the words, the transcriptions and the pictures.

1. desert 2. (to) desert 3. dessert

a. ___ /dɪˈzərt/ b. ___ /ˈdɛzərt/ c. ___ /dɪˈzərt/

d. ___

e. ___

f. ___

133 Exercise 3: The "ss" in these words is pronounced /z/. Listen and repeat:

de**ss**ert – po**ss**e**ss**ive – sci**ss**ors – di**ss**olve

134 Exercise 4: Although there isn't a written vowel, the suffix "-sm" is pronounced as a syllable (/zəm/). For example, the only difference between *prism* /ˈprɪzəm/ and *prison* /ˈprɪzən/ is the final sound (/m/ or /n/): both have two syllables. Pay attention to the secondary stress that precedes the suffix. Listen and repeat:

tóurì**sm** – cómmunì**sm**– péssimì**sm** – pátriotì**sm** – enthúsià**sm**

135 Exercise 5: Practice /z/ in these sentences. Repeat.

James **is** very po**ss**essive of his de**ss**ert.
Terrori**sm** tri**es** to di**ss**olve capitali**sm**.
Charl**es** alway**s** do**es** a**s** he say**s**.
The**se** bu**s**inessmen have enough ideali**sm** to build a re**s**ort.

Zoom in

136 Exercise 1: Repeat these contrasting words.

/s/	/z/
ice	eyes
spice	spies
loss	laws
price	prize
face	phase
loose	lose
once	ones
race	raise
advice	advise
niece	knees

Pay attention to these forms of address:
Miss /mɪs/ – Miss /s/ Adams
Ms. /mɪz/ – Ms. /z/ Adams

137 Exercise 2: The pronunciation of some words changes depending on the part of speech they belong to. Listen and compare:

noun / adjective – final /s/	verb – final /z/
abuse	to abuse
use	to use
excuse	to excuse
house	to house
close	to close

138 Exercise 3: Circle the /s/ sounds and underline the /z/ sounds in the words in bold type.

What's the **use** of buying it if you don't **use** it?
Close one of **these** windows and sit **close** to me.
Excuse us, but **this** isn't a good **excuse**.
You shouldn't **house** a pet in your **house**.
If you let it **loose**, you might **lose** it.

Attention:
this /ðɪs/ – this /s/ egg
these /ði:z/ – these /z/ eggs

Notice that the vowel sounds in *this* and *these* are different.

Now listen and correct. Read the sentences in pairs.

Stay tuned

139 Listen and circle the word you hear.

1. Could you tell me what the price / prize is?
2. This is the first face / phase we've discussed.
3. Can you race / raise your brother?
4. Everyone could see the ice / eyes.
5. I want to get those once / ones.

/fəˈnætɪk fər fəˈnɛtɪks/

Find these words in the puzzle:

/lu:s/
/dɪˈzərt/
/sɛz/
/ˈdʒɛnrəs/
/ˈaɪlənd/

/streɪt/
/ˈprɪzəm/
/ˈsɪzərz/
/bʌs/
/ðɛrz/

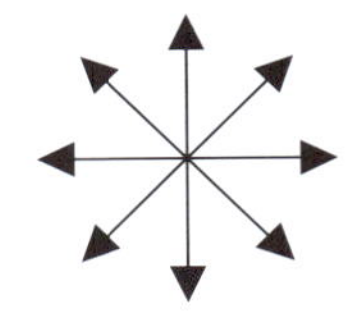

A	E	R	T	H	I	O	L	L	S	T	R	A	I	G	H	T
K	I	J	N	L	O	O	S	E	V	C	F	T	H	O	U	H
S	E	Z	O	R	E	S	N	I	O	P	L	Z	S	V	B	O
E	N	D	I	V	O	L	P	R	A	S	O	N	S	Z	A	Q
Q	W	E	R	T	Y	D	I	O	P	P	A	S	C	D	F	G
K	L	Z	X	C	V	E	N	M	M	E	T	E	I	R	N	I
C	R	O	S	D	E	S	S	E	R	T	A	I	S	N	O	S
E	C	R	A	F	M	E	O	T	B	O	N	G	S	T	I	N
S	Q	U	E	G	L	R	I	Z	I	B	A	S	O	A	I	L
U	T	E	A	H	C	T	E	R	S	T	U	D	R	E	N	T
B	K	L	O	I	N	G	E	V	I	G	R	X	S	T	Y	N
T	D	A	I	D	E	T	P	P	H	A	N	M	D	S	I	M
U	N	I	V	N	R	T	Y	C	R	O	L	A	S	A	Y	S
O	E	E	T	A	U	I	O	P	L	I	L	K	J	H	G	F
A	S	F	C	L	A	Q	X	S	W	T	S	R	F	V	B	N
B	R	A	N	S	N	H	A	P	E	D	R	M	O	M	Y	L
Q	A	Z	X	I	W	E	E	D	C	V	S	R	I	E	H	T
D	U	E	R	G	H	T	E	R	L	U	A	G	H	B	Y	C
S	K	E	I	T	B	O	R	D	G	E	N	E	R	O	U	S

Wrap up

Go back to **Think about it** and go over the questions again. Then check your answers in the **Answer Key**.

Unit 8 – Semi-Vowels: /w/ and /y/

Think about it

Exercise 1: Write *true* or *false*.

1. The words *ear* and *year* are pronounced the same way. ___
2. ***U**mbrella* and ***u**niform* start with the same sound. ___
3. *Would* and *wood* are pronounced the same way. ___
4. The semi-vowels /y/ and /w/ are never stressed. ___

Exercise 2: Pronounce these words and underline the /y/ and /w/ sounds.

Europe	uniform	quite	language
cure	year	equal	one
million	university	liquid	persuade

What's the difference between /y/ and /i:/? And between /w/ and /u:/?

Don't look at the **Answer Key** now! Study the unit to the end and then check your answers.

Close up

/y/ is usually spelled with "y" in initial position. It can also be spelled with a "u" in initial and medial position in words like *uniform* or *confusion*.

Zoom in

140 Exercise 1: Listen and repeat.

yesterday – **y**acht – **y**ellow
universe – **u**nicorn – **u**nion
c**u**te – h**u**ge – conf**u**se – c**u**rious

141 Exercise 2: Here are some other spellings of /y/.

v**iew** – f**ew** – p**ew**ter
Europe – **eu**calyptus
b**eau**ty – b**eau**tiful
mill**i**on – famil**i**ar – pavil**i**on

142 Exercise 3: Repeat these sentences:

Yesterday there was a h**u**ge conf**u**sion on my **y**acht.
Eugene is c**u**rious about **Eu**ropean political v**ie**ws.
M**u**riel gets f**u**rious when people arg**u**e over b**eau**ty.
A **u**nicorn is a c**u**te and p**u**re individ**u**al.

Close up

Umbrella and ***uniform*** start with the same letter, but we say ***an*** *umbrella*, and ***a*** *uniform*. *Umbrella* starts with a vowel sound (/ʌ/), but *uniform* starts with a semi-vowel (/y/). Before /y/ we use the article *a*. So you say *a unicorn*, *a university, a European country*, etc.

Compare:

an uncle – ***a*** union
an egg – ***a*** eucalyptus

Because ***a*** x ***an*** is taught in grammar books, people might think this is a grammar rule. Words such as *hour* and *university* are listed as exceptions due to their written form. If we consider the ***sound***, this rule has no exceptions.

Zoom in

143 Exercise 1: /y/ is not difficult for Brazilian students to pronounce, except when it comes before an /iː/ or /ɪ/, because they are very similar sounds. Words like *year* and *ear* often get confused. Try getting to the sound like this: say *ya-ye-yi*. Then say *ya-ye-year*. Repeat.

/yiː/ – /yiː/ – **y**east – **y**ield
/yɪ/ – /yɪ/ – **y**ear – **y**earbook – **Y**iddish

144 Exercise 2: Repeat these sentences.

Yuri signed his **y**earbook in **Y**iddish.
Ulysses **u**sed a lot of **y**east last **y**ear.

Get your tongue around it

145 Exercise 1: Repeat these words:

ear – **y**ear

Exercise 2: Complete these sentences using the correct form of *ear* or *year*.

1. Donkeys have long ___.
2. 1966 was a beautiful ___.
3. When you take a shower, don't forget to wash your ___.
4. Van Gogh had only one ___.
5. I've been living in São Paulo for many ___.
6. My son has been at school for three ___.
7. When you swim, protect your ___.
8. 365 days is the same as a ___.

146 Now close your books and repeat the sentences above.

147 Notice these two possible pronunciations. Listen:

		/yu:/	/u:/
/n/	new	/nyu:/	/nu:/
/t/	student	/ˈstyu:dənt/	/ˈstu:dənt/
/d/ + /y/	duty	/ˈdyu:ti/	/ˈdu:ti/
/s/	consume	/kənˈsyu:m/	/kənˈsu:m/
/θ/	enthusiasm	/ɛnˈðyu:zɪˌæzəm/	/ɛnˈðu:zɪˌæzəm/

/yu:/ is usually used by British English speakers, while most American English speakers use /u:/.

Close up

Unlike when you pronounce a vowel, when you say the semivowels /y/ and /w/, your tongue glides, moving from one place to another.

Note that /w/ is usually spelled with "w," but it can also be spelled with "u" in medial position as in *quiet*.

Zoom in

148 Exercise 1: Listen and repeat:

what* – **w**ild – **w**ell – **wh**ere*
a**w**ake – over**w**eight – s**w**ing – d**w**arf – t**w**in
q**u**ick – q**u**iz
lang**u**age – pers**u**ade

149 Exercise 2: Repeat these sentences:

The **w**ild ling**u**ist inq**u**ired about the g**u**acamole.
Be**w**are of your **w**aist – you're a little over**w**eight.
The t**w**in d**w**arfs s**w**ung on the s**w**ing.

150 Exercise 3: /w/ is not a hard sound for Brazilian students, except when it comes before an /u:/ or /ʊ/ because they are very similar sounds. Repeat these words:

would/**w**ood – **w**ool – **w**olf – **w**oman

> Pay attention to the irregular spelling of *one*.
> It sounds like the past tense of *win*, *won*.
> one = won /wʌn/
> once /wʌns/

151 Exercise 4: Repeat these phrases.

would you?
one **w**oman
once a **w**olf
wood or **w**ool?

* In some varieties, there's aspiration before the /w/: /hw/.

In context

152 Exercise 1: Listen to this paragraph.

Once upon a time, there **w**as a **w**oman and a **w**olf. The **w**oman **w**anted to skin the **w**olf to make a s**w**eater, and the **w**olf **w**anted to eat up the **w**oman. **O**ne **w**inter day, the **w**olf and the **w**oman met under a **w**illow tree. They looked at **o**ne another for **o**ne minute. Then the **w**olf said, "I'm hungry. That's **w**hy I **w**ant to eat you." The **w**oman said, "I'm cold. That's **w**hy I **w**ant to skin you." The **w**olf said, "I can get some **w**ood for you and light you a fire. You'll be **w**arm." Then the **w**oman said, "I can cook for you and you **w**on't be hungry any more." **W**ith that, they became lifelong friends, and lived happily ever after.

Read the paragraph in pairs. Then close your books and retell the story.

153 The Silent Corner

The "w" is silent in these words:

ans~~w~~er – s~~w~~ord
~~w~~ho – ~~w~~hose – ~~w~~hole
~~w~~rite – ~~w~~rinkle – ~~w~~rap
~~w~~rist – ~~w~~rong – ~~w~~restle

Exercise 2: Three of the words above have homophones. Write the pairs.

____________________ ____________________
____________________ ____________________
____________________ ____________________

/fəˈnætɪk fər fəˈnɛtɪks/

✎ Decipher the message.

/wʌns yu: pɜrˈsweɪd yʊrəˈpi:ən ˈwɪmən tə wɛr ˈsʌmθɪŋ ðə rɛst əv ðə wɜrld wɪl ˈfɑloʊ/

____

____

Fun time

✎ Exercise 1: This is a fun way of looking at some old sayings. Match the two parts of these one-line jokes:

1. We are born naked, wet and hungry.
2. Where there's a will,
3. Always remember you're unique,
4. When everything's coming your way,
5. By the time we realize our parents were right,
6. We have enough youth,
7. When you don't know what you are doing,

a. ( ) do it neatly.
b. ( ) we have children who think we're wrong.
c. ( ) I want to be in it.
d. ( ) you're in the wrong lane.
e. ( ) just like everyone else.
f. ( ) how about a fountain of smart?
g. ( ) Then things get worse.

✎ Exercise 2: Underline the semi-vowel sounds.

Wrap up

Go back to **Think about it** and go over the questions again. Then check your answers in the **Answer Key**.

Unit 9 – "-s" Endings

Think about it

Answer these questions.

1. When do you add an –s to the end of a word?
2. Does this –s always sound the same?
3. Analyze the –s ending in the words below. What does it sound like?

cat**s** – apple**s** – watch**es**

Don't look at the **Answer Key** now! Study the unit to the end and then check your answers.

Close up

We add –s at the end of words to form:

- Plurals
- The third person singular of verbs in the simple present
- Possessive ('s)
- Contractions (is/has)

Observe the chart:

Words ending in:	voiced sounds: add /z/	voiceless sounds: add /s/	sibilants: add /ɪz/*
Plurals	boys /bɔɪz/	cups /kʌps/	glasses /ˈglæsɪz/
Verbs in the 3rd person singular	lives /lɪvz/	takes /teɪks/	watches /ˈwɑtʃɪz/
Possessives	girl's /gɜrlz/	student's /ˈstu:dənts/	Max's /ˈmæksɪz/
Contractions	she's /ʃi:z/	Jeff's /dʒɛfs/	judge's /ˈdʒʌdʒɪz/

The –s ending will sound different depending on the sound that precedes it.

- After a voiced sound, add another voiced sound: /z/;
- After a voiceless sound, add another voiceless sound: /s/;
- After sibilants (/s/, /z/, /ʃ/, /ʒ/, /tʃ/, /dʒ/), add /ɪz/.

> This is not really a *rule*; it's just a description of what we do naturally when we speak. It's **easier** to add a similar sound. In the case of sibilants, we add a vowel between the sibilants to make the transition to /z/ more comfortable.

* /əz/ is also possible.

Zoom in

154 Exercise 1: These nouns end in voiceless sounds. They make their plural and possessive forms by adding an /s/ sound. Listen and repeat.

cap**s** – lak**es** – kit**es** – cuff**s**
Nick**'s** – wife**'s** – assistant**'s**

Most speakers simplify the plural of the word *month* and say only /mʌnts/ or even /mʌns/.

155 Exercise 2: Repeat these sentences, linking the sounds, like this:

plates are = plate sar

Matt**'s** plate**s** are on the desk**s**.
The vet**'s** cat**s** attacked my parrot**s**.
The insect**s** ate the president**'s** book**s**.
Jeff**'s** invitation wasn't delivered because the cop**'s** address was missing.

Get your tongue around it

156 Exercise 1: Listen to the words and put them in the correct place in the sentence. Remember to link the sounds and to stress the **verb**. Follow the example.

Model: *He never **likes** it.*
You: *He never **likes** it. = like sit* (repetition)
Model: (*take*)
You: *He never **takes** it.* = take sit
Model: *He never **takes** it.* (repetition)

Do it mentally (in silence) first. Then play the track again and do it orally.

drink – hit – type – get – make – wipe – laugh at

Exercise 2: Work in pairs. Monitor each other. Say the contracted form of these verbs in the sentence. The "s" is pronounced /s/ in all cases.

Student A: Janet is away.
Student B: *Janet's away.* = *Janet saway*

Don't forget that *has* is only contracted when it's an auxiliary verb!

The pilot has arrived.
The book is on the table.
My heart is Eric's.
Biff has amused me.
Mick is American.
My wife has eaten lunch.
The pope has asked for peace.
The cake is old.

Zoom in

157 Exercise 1: These nouns end in voiced sounds and make their plural and possessive by adding a /z/ sound. Listen and repeat:

day**s** – citie**s** – dog**s** – son**s** – car**s**
Joe**'s** – girl**'s** – boy**'s**

158 Exercise 2: Repeat these sentences, paying attention to the contractions. They are pronounced /z/.

Sheila**'s** arrived with Tim'**s** aunt.
My dog**'s** eleven year**s** old.
The doctor**'s** aide**'s** assured me swimming**'s** awesome.
Jill**'s** umbrella**s** are old.

Get your tongue around it

In pairs, look at Jack and Jill's mother's calendar and have a conversation as in the example, substituting the verbs. The letters "s" in bold are all pronounced /z/.

Bill: *When doe**s** your mother drive you to school?*
Jack: *She drive**s** us to school on Monday**s**.*

Mon	Tue	Wed	Thu	Fri	Sat	Sun
drive us to school	*see a therapist*	*study English*	*clean our room*	*call our grandmother*	*sing in a choir*	*read us a story*

Zoom in

159 Exercise 1: Nouns ending in sibilants (/s/, /z/, /ʃ/, /ʒ/, /tʃ/, /dʒ/) make their plural by adding /ɪz/. Listen and pay attention to the number of syllables.

> Due to the fact that you're adding an extra vowel, you add an extra **syllable**.

1 syllable	2 syllables
blouse /s/	blous**es** /sɪz/
rose /z/	ros**es** /zɪz/
watch /tʃ/	watch**es** /tʃɪz/
bridge /dʒ/	bridg**es** /dʒɪz/

Repeat the words above as a class. Tap for each syllable.

160 Exercise 2: Listen and repeat. Note that these one-syllable verbs have two syllables in the third person singular.

John never catch**es** a cold.
Bob coach**es** eight teams.
Patty chang**es** eleven blous**es** a day.
Sue pass**es** out when she sneez**es** a lot.
Sid teach**es** algebra.
Dave watch**es** all the games on TV.

Get your tongue around it

✎ Practice /ɪz/. In pairs, look at the pictures and describe what you see.

Liz's earrings

1. ______________________________

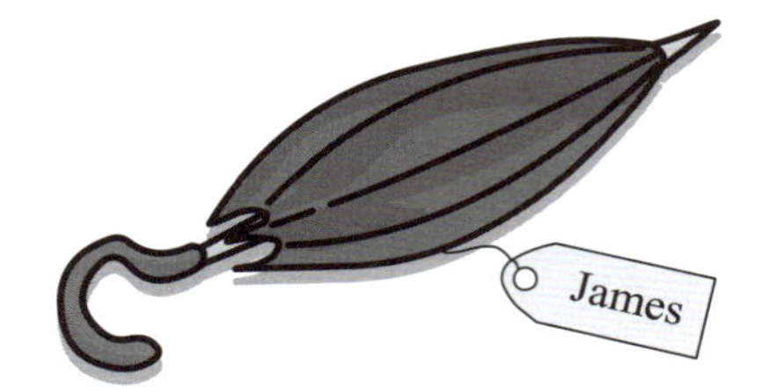

2. ______________________________

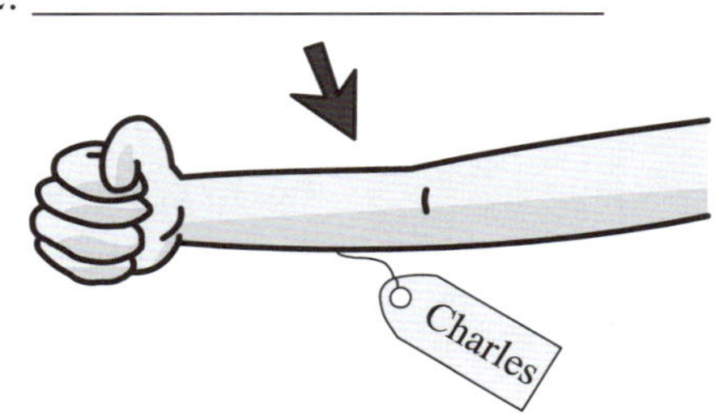

3. ______________________________

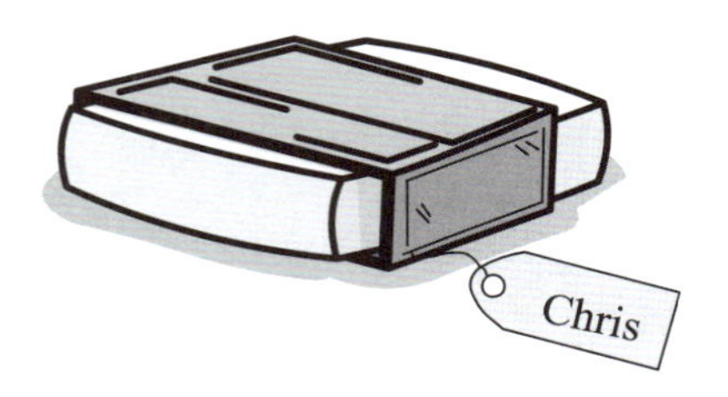

4. ______________________________

5. ______________________________

6. ______________________________

Stay tuned

161 Exercise 1: Listen to these words and circle the –s ending you hear.

1. /s/ /z/ /ɪz/
2. /s/ /z/ /ɪz/
3. /s/ /z/ /ɪz/
4. /s/ /z/ /ɪz/
5. /s/ /z/ /ɪz/
6. /s/ /z/ /ɪz/
7. /s/ /z/ /ɪz/
8. /s/ /z/ /ɪz/
9. /s/ /z/ /ɪz/
10. /s/ /z/ /ɪz/

Exercise 2: Pronounce the words below and check the correct column.

	add a sound	**add a syllable**
passes		x
hopes	x	
kisses		
snake's		
goes		
massages		
Kate's		
catches		
caves		
judge's		
noses		
studies		

Work with a classmate. Compare your answers and make up a conversation using some of the words above.

Conversation

162 Exercise 1: Listen to this interview, paying attention to the final –s sounds.

A: So, you are Mike Jackman**'s** assistant. Can you tell us some secret**s** about his everyday life?

B: Oh, sure. Mike**'s** been doing the same thing**s** for year**s**! He wake**s** up at 1:00 pm, and he take**s** a very long shower. He always sing**s** in the shower! Then he come**s** downstairs and eat**s** a big breakfast with his four dog**s**. He watch**es** the 3 o'clock program on MTV and then he teach**es** Albert, his parrot, to speak Italian.

A: His parrot speak**s** Italian?

B: Most parrot**s** are able to speak, but Albert speak**s** three language**s**!

Exercise 2: Practice the conversation in pairs.

Exercise 3: What else does Mr. Jackman do? Write one more eccentric thing and read it to the class. The rest of the class should raise their right hand if the final –s is pronounced /s/, their left hand if it is pronounced /z/, or both hands if it is pronounced /ɪz/.

Mike Jackman __________________________________ *every day.*

In context

163 Listen to what Bill does every morning. Write the verbs you hear in the correct columns.

/s/	/z/	/ɪz/

Interview a classmate about things he does every morning (at least five things). Sit with another classmate and report what you heard. Use the third person singular.

/fəˈnætɪk fər fəˈnɛtɪks/

Transcribe the words you practiced in *Stay Tuned*.

passes	/ˈpæsɪz/	massages	
hopes		Kate's	
studies		catches	
kisses		caves	
snake's		judge's	
goes		noses	

Fun time

In groups of three, play *Shopping Carts*. You are at the supermarket, and you have to fill three shopping carts according to the pronunciation of the –s ending. The first group to fill the carts correctly gets 5 points.

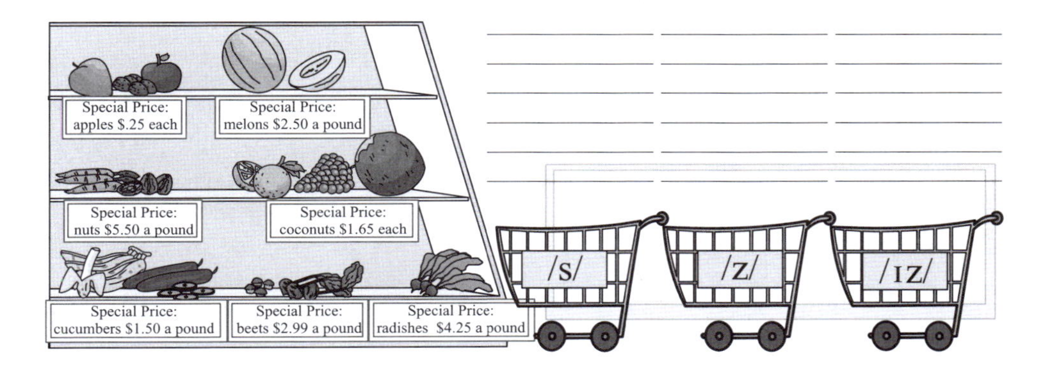

Wrap up

Go back to **Think about it** and go over the questions again. Then check your answers in the **Answer Key**.

Unit 10 – Final -ed

Think about it

Exercise 1: Pronounce these three groups of verbs and match them to the correct pronunciation of –ed ending.

/?/	/?/		/?/
work**ed**	begg**ed**	bang**ed**	paint**ed**
typ**ed**	arriv**ed**	bath**ed**	want**ed**
watch**ed**	robb**ed**	plann**ed**	aid**ed**
wash**ed**	play**ed**	seem**ed**	hat**ed**

/t/

/ɪd/

/d/

Exercise 2: Identify the number of syllables in the following pairs of verbs:

1. a. work ( )
   b. worked ( )
2. a. study ( )
   b. studied ( )
3. a. need ( )
   b. needed ( )
4. a. smile ( )
   b. smiled ( )
5. a. want ( )
   b. wanted ( )
6. a. help ( )
   b. helped ( )

Don't look at the **Answer Key** now! Study the unit to the end and then check your answers.

Close up

These are the pronunciations of the –ed ending:

Verbs ending in:

voiced sounds: add /d/	voiceless sounds: add /t/	/t/ or /d/: add /ɪd/
arrive /əˈraɪv/ arrived /əˈraɪvd/	look /lʊk/ look /lʊkt/	need /ni:d/ needed /ˈni:dɪd/
study /ˈstʌdi/ studied /ˈstʌdid/	hope /hoʊp/ hoped /hoʊpt/	print /prɪnt/ printed /ˈprɪntɪd/

Zoom in

164 Exercise 1: The –ed in the following verbs is pronounced /t/. Listen and repeat. Attention: all these verbs are one-syllable words.

/pt/	/kt/	/ft/	/st/	/ʃt/	/tʃt/
stopp**ed**	talk**ed**	laugh**ed**	mess**ed**	crash**ed**	match**ed**
wip**ed**	lik**ed**	stuff**ed**	fax**ed**	fish**ed**	watch**ed**
typ**ed**	pick**ed**	goof**ed**	danc**ed**	wish**ed**	fetch**ed**

165 Exercise 2: Repeat the base form and past tense form tapping once for each. Follow the model.

stop – stopped
dance – danced
look – looked

wash – washed
watch – watched
laugh – laughed

166 These words sound the same. They are homophones.

passed = past
missed = mist
packed = pact
guessed = guest
paced = paste

In context

167 Exercise 1: Repeat these phrases.

asked her to go /t/	skipped on her way /t/
picked a few flowers /t/	dressed up /t/
fetched her basket /t/	talked her out of /t/
walked a long way /t/	relaxed a little /t/
packed it with fruit /t/	jumped a puddle /t/

168 Exercise 2: Listen to the first part of the fairy tale *Little Red Riding Hood*.

Little Red Riding Hood walk**ed** a long way to her Grandmother's house every day. One day her mother ask**ed** her to go there early in the morning, so she fetch**ed** her basket, pack**ed** it with fruit and candy, and skipp**ed** on her way to the forest. She pick**ed** a few flowers, jump**ed** a puddle or two and relax**ed** a little on the way, when a Big Bad Wolf dress**ed** up as an angel surfac**ed** from behind the bushes and talk**ed** her out of taking the path by the river.

Repeat the paragraph after the model.

Get your tongue around it

Exercise 1: In pairs, say these sentences in the past, making the necessary changes. Pay attention to the final /t/ sound and link it to the following vowel. Follow the example.

Student: *He picks up his wife every day.*
He picked up his wife yesterday.
/t/

1. I wish upon a star every night.
2. He works a lot every year.
3. She types a letter every day.
4. They watch a silly cartoon every morning.
5. We miss our friend every weekend.
6. We wash our clothes every Saturday.

Exercise 2: In pairs, match the columns. Pronounce the past tense as clusters. For example: /pt/, /st/. Don't add an extra syllable.

1. marched	( )	a. our car
2. watched	( )	b. Everest's highest point
3. kissed	( )	c. at the flowers
4. saved	( )	d. one hundred miles
5. tipped	( )	e. Anna and Beth
6. parked	( )	f. a boring movie
7. coughed	( )	g. eight hundred dollars
8. reached	( )	h. a lot
9. looked	( )	i. a waiter

169 Exercise 3: Listen and check your answers. Try to speak along with the model.

Zoom in

170 Exercise 1: The –ed ending in the following verbs is pronounced /d/. Listen and repeat. Don't add an extra syllable.

/bd/	/gd/	/vd/	/md/	/nd/	/ld/
brib**ed** grabb**ed**	jogg**ed** lagg**ed**	liv**ed** serv**ed**	nam**ed** climb**ed**	open**ed** train**ed**	roll**ed** smell**ed**
/rd/	/zd/	/ðd/	/ŋd/	/dʒ/d/	vowel + /d/
appear**ed** scor**ed**	confus**ed** rais**ed**	breath**ed** bath**ed**	long**ed** bang**ed**	encourag**ed** merg**ed**	cri**ed** show**ed**

Exercise 2: Write homophones for these verbs in the past.

allowed = ______________________________
banned = ______________________________
billed = ______________________________
fined = ______________________________
sighed = ______________________________
tied = ______________________________

171 Exercise 3: Now say the past tense of these verbs. Follow the example and tap for each syllable. Don't add an extra syllable.

Model: *save*
You: *saved* /seɪvd/
Model: *saved*
You: *saved* (repetition)

beg – bang – arrive – rob – plan – play – seem – realize
change – call – share – massage – marry

In context

Exercise 1: In pairs, practice the past tense of these verbs and put them in the correct columns. Remember: the –ed is pronounced /d/. Don't add an extra syllable.

warn – stroll – prepare – prefer – open – love – live – hurry – fear
disobey – devour – arrive – hum – worry

1 syllable	2 syllables	3 syllables

Exercise 2: Read the second part of the fairy tale *Little Red Riding Hood* and complete the paragraph with the past tense of the verbs in the box.

Little Red Riding Hood (1) ________________ as she (2) ________________ along the path of the forest. She (3) ________________ this path, and (4) ____________ it to the one along the river, but her mother had (5) __________ her it was dangerous, as a wolf (6) ________________ in the area. She (7) ________________ about the fact that she had (8) ________________ her mother, but she (9) ________________ no wolf. Meanwhile, the wolf had (10) ________________ to Grandmother's house and (11) ________________ there before Little Red. Grandmother (12) ________________ the door and was appalled to see a wolf standing there. The wolf (13) ________________ Grandmother and (14) ________________ himself to attack Little Red.

172 Listen and check your answers. Then read the paragraph with a friend, paying attention to the /d/ endings. Remember to link /d/ and the next vowel when appropriate. Monitor each other.

Get your tongue around it

173 Your mother is telling you to do certain things. Substitute the verbs as in the example. Remember to stress the **verb**!

Model: *Change your shirt.*
You: *But I've already* ***changed*** *it!*
/d/
Model:: *But I've already* ***changed*** *it!*
You: *But I've already* ***changed*** *it! (repetition)*

Close the window.
Study English.
Comb your hair.
Mail the letter.
Try the food.
Move your bed.
Order a pizza.
Bathe the cat.

Zoom in

174 Exercise 1: Listen and write down the number of syllables.

1. accept ( )
2. accepted ( )
3. pretend ( )
4. pretended ( )
5. fade ( )
6. faded ( )
7. investigate ( )
8. investigated ( )

175 Exercise 2: Practice the past tense of verbs ending in /t/ or /d/. The –ed is pronounced as an extra syllable. Repeat and tap your fingers for each syllable.

one syllable	two syllables
last	last**ed**
paste	past**ed**
want	want**ed**
waste	wast**ed**
list	list**ed**

two syllables	three syllables
accept	accept**ed**
subtract	subtract**ed**
protest	protest**ed**
elect	elect**ed**
digest	digest**ed**

176 Exercise 3: When /t/ and /d/ are in unstressed syllables between vowels or between /r/ and a vowel, they are usually pronounced as a flap [ɾ] in American English. Listen and repeat.

ha**t**ed – invi**t**ed – visi**t**ed
a**dd**ed – nee**d**ed – deci**d**ed
forwar**d**ed – recor**d**ed – suppor**t**ed

177 Exercise 4: Practice these verbs followed by *it*. Remember to stress the verb.

I háted it. I néeded it. I recórded it. I suppórted it.

178 Exercise 5: For many native speakers, the words *winner* and *winter* sound the same. The /t/ can be omitted when it follows /n/ in an unstressed syllable. Compare.

I **printed** the document.
Graham Bell **invented** the telephone.
I never **wanted** to learn German.

You don't have to pronounce these words this way, but recognizing them is important.

179 Exercise 6: ***Adjectives*** that end in –ed don't follow the rule. The –ed is pronounced as an extra syllable. Listen and repeat.

2-syllable words: wretch**ed** – wick**ed** – crook**ed** – ragg**ed** – nak**ed**
3-syllable words: cross-legg**ed** – belov**ed**

In context

180 Listen to the last part of the story.

The wolf pretend**ed** he was Grandmother and invit**ed** Little Red in. When Little Red not**ed** that his eyes, ears, nose and mouth were too big, the wolf assault**ed** her. She shout**ed** and expect**ed** to be heard by someone. A hunter decid**ed** to check what that noise was all about. He hunt**ed** down the wolf, wound**ed** him and defend**ed** Little Red. The little girl almost faint**ed** with joy when she saw that her grandmother was alive inside the wolf, and she understood that her disobedience result**ed** in something terrible. She decid**ed** never to disobey her mother again.

Read the paragraph along with the model, paying attention to the /ɪd/ endings.

Stay tuned

✎ Pronounce these verbs and circle the correct answer according to the –ed ending.

1. landed – ended – aided
a. /t/
b. /d/
c. /ɪd/

2. waxed – cuffed – pushed
a. /t/
b. /d/
c. /ɪd/

3. craved – spoiled – teethed
a. /t/
b. /d/
c. /ɪd/

4. subbed – revealed – studied
a. /t/
b. /d/
c. /ɪd/

5. sentenced – marked – itched
a. /t/
b. /d/
c. /ɪd/

6. listened – answered – questioned
a. /t/
b. /d/
c. /ɪd/

7. founded – cited – quoted
a. /t/
b. /d/
c. /ɪd/

8. developed – masked – locked
a. /t/
b. /d/
c. /ɪd/

In groups, make sentences with some of these verbs. Read the sentences to the class to check the correct pronunciation of the –ed endings.

Get your tongue around it

181 Repeat these contrasting sentences.

I cross a big river to get here.	a. Really? Every day?
I crossed a big river to get here.	b. Weren't you afraid?

I really appreciate the things people paint on walls.	a. Yes. I love graffiti too.
I really appreciate the things people painted on walls	b. Pre-historic drawings are really amazing.

They amaze us with their magic tricks.	a. Well, they are professional magicians.
They amazed us with their magic tricks.	b. You mean at the party last night?

We never arrive on time.	a. Why can't you ever be punctual?
We never arrived on time.	b. Why were you always late?

I watch art movies on TV.	a. When do you do that?
I watched art movies on TV.	b. I watched them last night too.

I attend eight lectures.	a. A day?
I attended eight lectures.	b. Oh, were they interesting?

Work in pairs. Go back to the exercise. Student A says one of the sentences. Student B identifies it (present or past) and responds accordingly. Follow the example.

Student A: I cross a big river to get here.
Student B: Really? Every day?

/fəˈnætɪk fər fəˈnɛtɪks/

Identify the verbs and transcribe the past forms.

plan	/plæn/		/rɪˈlæks/		/ni:d/
	/plænd/				
	/wɑʃ/		/əˈraɪv/		/heɪt/
	/θæŋk/		/rɪˈkɔrd/		/ˈmɛʒər/
	/klaɪm/		/prəˈtɛst/		/bri:ð/

Fun time

Fairy tales are an important part of most people's childhood. They are also a great way to practice the verbs in the past! In groups, choose one of the following stories. Then identify the –ed endings.

Cinderella	The Three Little Pigs	Snow White and the Seven Dwarfs
die	construct	look
raise	want	ask
invite	huff	clean
prohibit	puff	work
appear	destroy	discover
dance	climb	offer
escape	place	faint
live	play	marry

You have 5 minutes to recreate the story using all the verbs suggested in the order given. Then each group should tell their story to the class, who will check if all the verbs were pronounced correctly.

Part C
The English Vowels

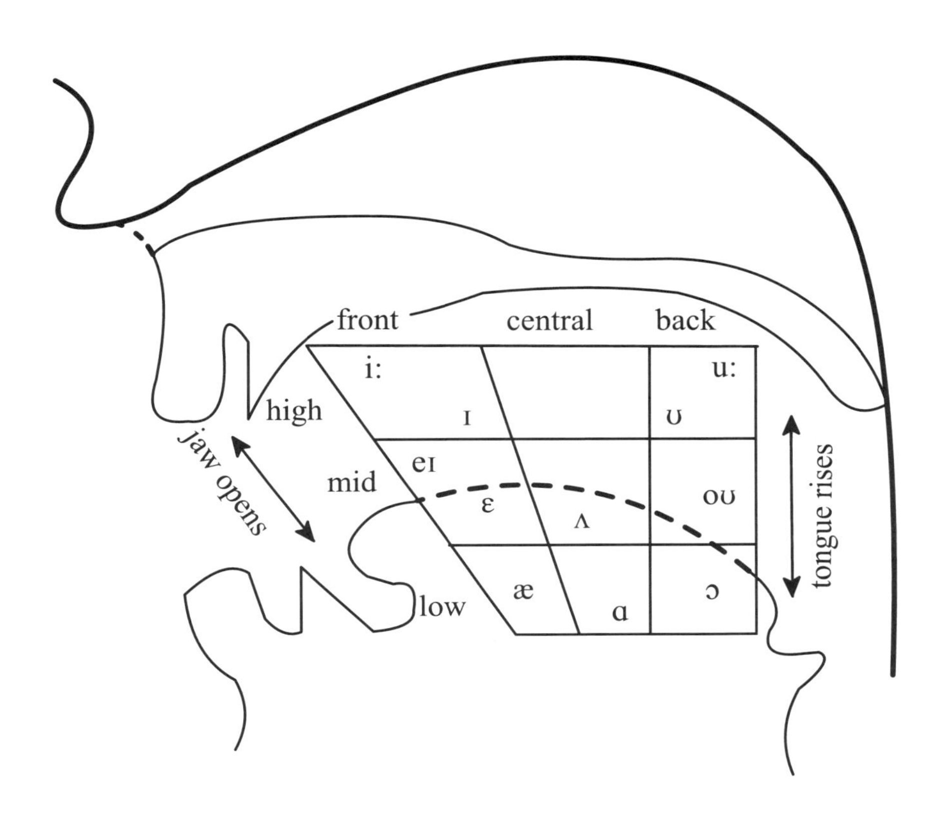

	Front	Central	Back
High	/i:/ as in *tea* /ɪ/ as in *big*		/u:/ as in *blue* /ʊ/ as in *book*
Mid	/eɪ/ as in *pay* /ɛ/ as in *get*	/ɜr/ as in *bird* /ʌ/ as in *but* /ə/ an in ***a**bout*	/oʊ/ as in *go*
Low	/æ/ as in cat	/ɑ/ as in *bar*, *not*	/ɔ/ as in *four*
	/aɪ/ as in *my*	/aʊ/as in *cow*	/ɔɪ/ as in *boy*

Intro – The Schwa Sound /ə/ and the Unstressed Syllable

Think about it

In small groups, discuss questions 1, 2 and 3 as you read. How much of this information is new to you?

1. What is /ə/?

The sound /ə/ is so important it has a name: schwa. Some people wonder where the name comes from. It's originally from Hebrew, meaning *nought* or *absence of vowel*. It's also said to be derived from two German words

Schwaches Ausspruch
weak pronunciation

An interesting feature to keep in mind is that /ə/ is the easiest sound to produce: if we just open our mouth a little and emit voice, we will be pronouncing /ə/. The mouth is in neutral position. For being so easy to produce, it is the sound we automatically make when we think, "Uh..."

2. Why is /ə/ so important?

Because it is the most frequent sound in English. According to the chart of frequencies of English phonemes (Gimson, *An Introduction to the Pronunciation of English*, Arnold, 1980), /ə/ appears with a frequency of 10.74%.

3. Why is /ə/ so frequent in the English language?

Almost all unstressed syllables are /ə/. Analyze the pronunciation of this word:

/ə/ /ə/ /ə/
a v **á** i l a b l e (4 syllables, 3 /ə/)

Pronounce these words and mark the stressed syllable.

Brazilian	construction	jealous	minute	proportional
________	________	________	________	________

How many /ə/ can you count in each word? Write the number of /ə/ under each word above.

Close up

Take a look:

/ə/ /ə/	/ə/ /ə/	/ə/	/ə/	/ə/ /ə/ /ə/
Braz**í**lian	constr**ú**ction	j**éa**lous	m**í**nute	prop**ó**rtional

You see, except for the stressed syllable, all the other vowels are /ə/. It's important to notice that unstressed vowels are pronounced /ə/ no matter how they are spelled. In the example above we have /ə/ spelled *a*, *ia*, *o*, *io*, *ou* and *u*.

Look at this pair:

pr**ó**ject (noun) /ə/ X proj**é**ct (verb) /ə/

The /ə/ changes place because the stress changes.

Do you understand now the name schwa (weak pronunciation)?

Zoom in

183 Listen to these words. Mark the vowel in the stressed syllable and circle the /ə/.

Example: m**ó**th(e)r

kitchen	computer	confusion	famous
stomach	excellent	necklace	private

Close up

Learners don't realize there are so many /ə/ sounds in English and, consequently, don't produce them. They go by the written form, and pronounce the letter they see, as if the letter sounded as in Portuguese. For example:

	Typical wrong pronunciation	**Correct pronunciation**
ous in vari***ous***	/oʊz/	/əs/
pro in ***pro***duction	/pro/	/prə/
ion in illus***ion***	/on/	/ən/

Although /ə/ is the most frequent vowel sound in unstressed syllables, /ɪ/ can also occur. In the words below, they can be used interchangeably. You can say:

/ə/ /ɪ/ /ə/ /ɪ/ /ɪ/ /ə/ /ə/ /ə/ /ɪ/ /ɪ/
b**e**hind or b**e**hind   pr**e**fer or pr**e**fer   del**i**c**a**te or del**i**c**a**te or del**i**c**a**te

Likewise, /ʊ/ also occurs in unstressed syllables. You can say, for example,

/ʊ/ /ə/
t**o**day or t**o**day

> Note that *you* /yu:/ can be reduced to /yʊ/ or /yə/
> as in *See you*! /si: yə/
>
> Some dictionaries show this choice like this: behind /ɪ ə/ today /ʊ ə/
> beautiful /byu:tɪfʊl/ (ə ə)

The choice depends on the speaker, dialect or even situation. When people are tired, sleepy or even drunk, they produce more /ə/ sounds because it is the easiest sound to produce.

In summary, this is what usually occurs:

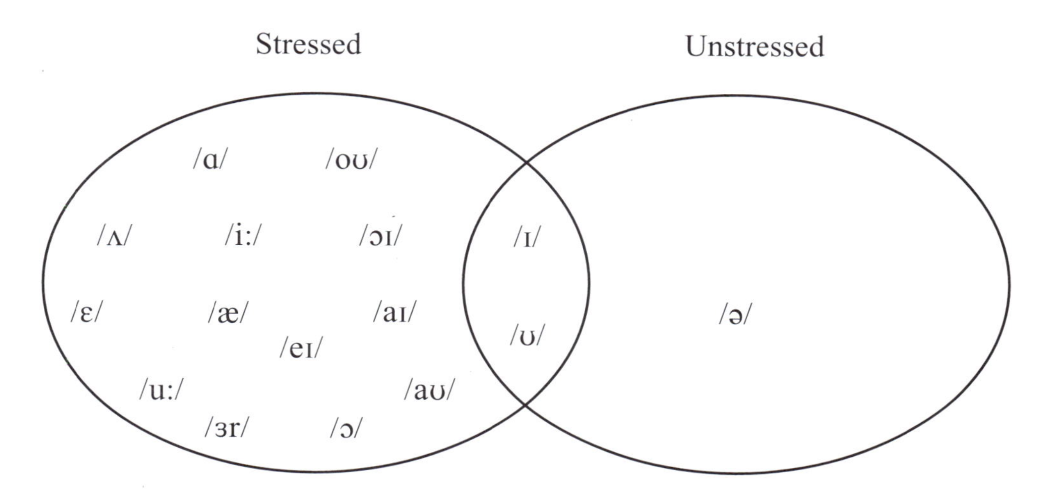

Zoom in

184 Don't jump to the extreme conclusion that all unstressed syllables are /ə/, /ɪ/ or /ʊ/. Do the next exercise in four steps.

1. Underline the vowel sounds to check how many syllables each word has. Watch out for the silent "e" at the end of some words.
2. Listen to the words below.
3. Mark the stressed syllable.
4. Indicate the vowel sound of the unstressed syllables.

	/aɪ/ /ə/ /i/	/æ/ /ə/
Example:	bi**ó**logy	advert**í**se

hypothesis	technology	justify	operator	female
organize	television	guarantee	teenager	acrobat

> We call ***silent e*** the letter *e* which is not pronounced at the end of words. It does not constitute a syllable, as in *like* (one syllable) and *language* (two syllables).

Close up

Different languages have different ways of showing hesitation to make time to think. In English, /ə/ is used for this purpose and is shown as *uh* in written language. In Portuguese, we make the final sound longer. We say, *Eu acho-o-o-o... Ele disse-e-e-e...*

Brazilians tend to transfer this behavior to English, getting bad results: *I think-i-i-i... His name is-z-z-z...* Native speakers do the following: *I think...uh...*

Zoom in

185 Let's practice hesitation with /ə/. Work in pairs. Ask each other the questions below and supply free responses, using one of the phrases given. Listen to these examples.

I don't know... uh...
Let me think... uh...
Well, let's see... uh...
I guess... uh...

1. Do you think computers will replace human beings in the future?
2. Who's the most wonderful person you know?
3. Where in the world would you like to spend the rest of your life?
4. Are you for or against same sex marriages? Why?
5. What's the best movie you have ever seen?
6. Was your city a better place to live 100 years ago?

Wrap up

You are not going to practice /ə/ in depth in this unit. You have been doing that without being aware of it while practicing the consonants and will continue doing it as you study the vowels. The important thing to remember is that **the vowel sound in most unstressed syllables is** /ə/.

Unit 1: /iː/ as in *tea* and /ɪ/ as in *big*

Think about it

Discuss these questions.

1. Do the words *hit* and *heat* sound the same?

2. Would you say that the Portuguese /i/ is the same as…
a. /iː/ as in *tea*
b. /ɪ/ as in *big*
c. neither

3.
a. What is the sound that can have all the spellings below? /______ /
b. Can you think of one example for each spelling?

ee	
ea	
e	
ey	
ei	
ie	
i	

Don't look at the **Answer Key** now! Study the unit to the end and then check your answers.

Close up

Because the Portuguese /i/ is between /iː/ and /ɪ/, many Brazilians don't differentiate the two sounds, so they pronounce *seat* and *sit* the same way, for instance. It's important to distinguish these sounds because each will form a different word. If you are not careful, you might inadvertently produce a word you don't mean.

/iː/ and /ɪ/ are usually called the long "i" and the short "i," respectively, but there's more to this difference than just duration. /iː/ is articulated higher in the mouth than /ɪ/. When you pronounce these sounds in this sequence:

↓
/iː/ English
/i/ Portuguese
/ɪ/ English

you'll notice that your jaw starts high and your mouth will open more and more as you go down. That means that /iː/ is pronounced higher in your mouth, followed by the Portuguese /i/ a little lower, and then /ɪ/.

/iː/ is also **tenser** than /ɪ/. The height causes the tongue to go up and the lips to spread more, yielding a tenser sound. When you take pictures, don't people tell you to say *cheese* to look like you're smiling? That's because you have to tense your muscles to spread your lips to say /iː/. When you relax your muscles and your mouth goes back to a more neutral position, then you articulate /ɪ/.

Zoom in

186 Exercise 1: Listen: /iː/ - /ɪ/ /iː/ - /ɪ/

/iː/	eat	seek	sleep	beat/beet	bean
/ɪ/	it	sick	slip	bit	been/bin

187 Exercise 2: Repeat these words with /iː/. Remember that this sound is long and tense, so "smile" as you pronounce it.

f**ee**t /fiːt/	s**ea**/s**ee** /siː/	**ea**t /iːt/
tr**ee** /triː/	b**ea**t/b**ee**t /biːt/	**ea**ch /iːtʃ/
kn**ee** /niː/	m**ea**t/m**ee**t /miːt/	sp**ea**k /spiːk/

Observe the words above and complete the statement:

The sound /iː/ is usually written with the letters ___ ___ or ___ ___.

188 Exercise 3: Notice other spellings for /iː/. Listen to these words.

b**e**	rec**ei**ve	bel**ie**ve
compl**e**te	conc**ei**ve	ach**ie**ve
h**e**	s**ei**ze	ch**ie**f
even	c**ei**ling	f**ie**ld
ego		p**ie**ce
Egypt		

189 Exercise 4: These are unusual spellings for /iː/. Listen and repeat:

sk**i**	mach**i**ne	k**ey**
v**i**sa	ch**i**c	p**eo**ple
magaz**i**ne	pol**i**ce	Ph**oe**nix

190 Exercise 5: When /iː/ occurs in final, non-stressed position, it is not as long. For this reason, we use the symbol /i/ without (ː), which indicates a long sound. Repeat these words:

merr**y** /ˈmɛri/	funn**y**	mon**ey**	mov**ie**	recip**e**
prett**y** /ˈprɪti/	sunn**y**	turk**ey**	calor**ie**	coff**ee**

191 Exercise 6: Repeat these phrases with /i:/ and /i/.

bel**ie**ve m**e**
s**ee** the pol**i**ce
gr**ee**n wh**ea**t f**ie**ld
extr**e**mel**y** wind**y**

an **eas**y recip**e**
m**ee**t m**e** at thr**ee**
sp**ea**k and l**ea**ve
coff**ee** or t**ea**

Think of more words with /i:/ or /i/ and write three more phrases or sentences. Read them aloud.

Close up

The short /ɪ/ is more similar to "ê" than to "i" in Portuguese. The sequence would be:

/i:/ English
/i/ Portuguese
/ɪ/ English
ê Portuguese

↓ We open our mouth in this direction.

When we pronounce /ɪ/, our muscles are **relaxed** (you don't "smile") and this sound is **short in duration**.

Zoom in

192 Exercise 1: Repeat these words with /ɪ/:

if - b**i**g – d**i**d – s**i**t
v**i**s**i**b**i**l**i**ty – **i**ns**i**p**i**d – t**i**m**i**d

193 Exercise 2: Repeat these phrases and short sentences.

a qu**i**ck k**i**ss
dr**i**nk m**i**lk
s**i**ck f**i**sh

h**i**s tr**i**p
if **i**t's **i**ll
s**i**nce spr**i**ng

Did Nick miss him?
If Bill sings, Bill will win.
Tim is the sixth on this list.

✎ Analyze the words in Exercises 1 and 2 and complete the statement:

The sound /ɪ/ is usually spelled with the letter ________________ between ________________ or in ________________ position followed by a ________________.

While /iː/ can have many different spellings,
/ɪ/ is much easier to identify. It's usually:
C i C = consonant + **i** + consonant

194 Exercise 3: Pay attention to the unusual spelling of /ɪ/ in these words:

The b**u**sinessman in **E**ngland was g**ui**lty.
The b**u**sy **E**nglish w**o**men were **i**n the b**ui**lding.
The t**y**pical s**y**stem has b**ee**n running pr**e**tty q**ui**ckly.

195 Exercise 4: We saw that "ee" and "ea" are the typical spellings for /iː/. But when these letters are followed by "r," the sound is /ɪr/. Listen and repeat.

near /nɪr/	**beer** /bɪr/
clear /klɪr/	**dear** / **deer** /dɪr/
cheer /tʃɪr/	**sheer** / **shear** /ʃɪr/
fear /fɪr/	**peer** /pɪr/

Also:

pier /pɪr/	**mere** /mɪr/
fierce /fɪrs/	**here** /hɪr/
weird /wɪrd/	sev**ere** /səˈvɪr/

196 Exercise 5: Repeat these sentences.

The b**eer** on your b**ear**d looks w**eir**d.
My d**ear**, don't f**ear** and dry your t**ear**.
Don't sh**ear** the d**eer** n**ear** h**ere**.

Close up

Some people believe that it's not important to worry about the difference between /iː/ and /ɪ/, as the context should solve any possible doubt. This can be true, but read these anecdotes:

I was in Honolulu looking at the sea admiring the view.
I have no idea why a girl slapped me in the face when I said to her:

What a beautiful /bɪtʃ/!

I was at the mall looking at bedspreads and linens, and
I was really surprised to get a nasty look just because I said:

Wow, look at this /ʃɪt/!

Words like *fit* and *feet*, *slip* and *sleep* only differ by one sound. They're called **minimal pairs**.

Zoom in

197 Exercise 1: Repeat these minimal pairs.

feet – fit	cheap – chip	steal/steel – still	beat/beet – bit
peak – pick	eat – it	heal/heel – hill	least – list

Try this exercise in pairs: articulate one of the words above, but silently, not making any sound. Your classmate will have to identify the "i" sound just looking at your mouth and say "long" or "short." If you articulate /i:/ and /ɪ/ correctly, that is, if you move your muscles the right way, and pay attention to duration, your classmate won't have to actually hear the sound to identify it.

Exercise 2: Circle the /i:/ and /i/ and underline the /ɪ/ in the sentences below.

Cindy and Rita are busy women, but they manage to keep fit.
Will Peter sit and listen?
Athletes wish the system weren't tricky.
Please dear, be clear.

198 Exercise 3: Now repeat the sentences above.

Stay tuned

199 Exercise 1: Listen and check the pictures according to what you hear.

1. a ______________

1. b ______________

2. a ________________

2. b ________________

3. a ________________

3. b ________________

4. a ________________

4. b ________________

5. a ________________

5. b ________________

Exercise 2: Listen again and write the sentences you hear.

Exercise 3: Now write the other possibility (the minimal pair).

Exercise 4: Work in pairs. Say a sentence and your friend points to the corresponding picture.

Fun time

Work in pairs. You have five minutes to list as many parts of the body as you can think of with /iː/ and /ɪ/. You can use both singular and plural words. The pair that gets the most correct words wins the game.

Clue: Think of the spelling rules when sorting the words.

/iː/		/ɪ/	

/fəˈnætɪk fər fəˈnɛtɪks/

✎ Now this is the big challenge! Transcribe the words corresponding to the parts of the body correctly.

1. /____/ 2. /_____/ 3. /_____/ 4. /_____/

5. /_____/ 6. /_____/ 7. /_____/ 8. /_____/

9. /_____/ 10. /_____/ 11. /_____/ 12. /_____/

Wrap up

Go back to **Think about it** and go over the questions again. Then check your answers in the **Answer Key**.

Unit 2: /ɛ/ as in *get* and /æ/ as in *cat*

Think about it

Discuss these questions.

1. Do you pronounce *man* and *men* the same way?

2. Do you think Brazilians have problems differentiating these sounds? Why (not)?

3. How is the sound /æ/ as in *cat* usually spelled?

4. Pronounce /ɛ/ as in *get* and /æ/ as in *cat*. Now pronounce *é* in Portuguese. Pay attention to how much you open your mouth to pronounce these three sounds. Now place /ɛ/, /æ/ and ***é*** in this scale.

a. ___ less open
b. ___ in between
c. ___ more open

Don't look at the **Answer Key** now! Study the unit to the end and then check your answers.

Close up

Portuguese has only one *é* sound. English has two and they're different from the Portuguese *é*, which is between /ɛ/ as in *get* and /æ/ as in *cat*.

So this is the scale:

less open:	/ɛ/ as in *egg*
in between:	Portuguese *é* as in *pé*
more open:	/æ/ as in *cat*

To produce these English sounds, follow these steps: Say *é* in Portuguese. Then close your lips a little and you will pronounce /ɛ/. Now, open your mouth to say *a* in Portuguese but don't say *a*, say *é*. That's the /æ/ sound.

Practice.

/ɛ/
é
/æ/

↓ open your mouth

Zoom in

Let's practice /ɛ/. Remember it's not as open as *é* in Portuguese. Follow the technique: Say *é*, close your lips a little and say, /ɛ/, /ɛ/, /ɛ/.

200 Exercise 1: Repeat these words. This is a **short sound**.

egg – **e**ver – **e**cho – **e**nd

201 Exercise 2: Repeat these phrases with /ɛ/.

wh**e**re **e**lse
r**e**dn**e**ck
g**e**t the t**e**st
s**e**nd t**e**n b**e**lls
dr**e**ss on the b**e**d
l**e**d the m**e**n

✎ Observe the words in Exercises 1 and 2 and complete the sentence:

The sound /ɛ/ can be spelled with the letter ________________ between ________________, or in initial position followed by a ________________.

> The letter *e* in initial position is also pronounced /ɛ/ in words with more than one syllable if the *e* is stressed and followed by a consonant.

202 Exercise 3: Repeat these words:

émpty	énergy	élbow
éducate	éngine	émbassy

203 Exercise 4: If *e* is **unstressed**, it's usually pronounced /ɪ/ or /ə/. Listen to these words.

enáble	**e**ffícient	**e**xámple
excúse	**e**ncóurage	**e**mérgency

204 Exercise 5: Here are some spellings of /ɛr/. Listen.

sh**are**	p**air**	t**ear**
c**are**	f**air**	b**ear**
prep**are**	d**air**y	p**ear**

205 Exercise 6: In these words, the spelling of /ɛ/ is atypical. Listen and repeat.

any	h**ea**ven	ag**ai**n	s**ay**s	fr**ie**nd	j**eo**pardize
m**a**ny	br**ea**d	ag**ai**nst	pr**ay**er	b**u**ry	l**eo**pard
	h**ea**vy	s**ai**d	m**ay**or	h**ei**r	L**eo**nard
	w**ea**ther			sc**a**rce	

> *Air* and *heir* are homophones.
> *The **heir** conditioned his driver to keep his car **air**-conditioned.*

Get your tongue around it

206 Some verbs change from /iː/ to /ɛ/ in the simple past. Listen and repeat.

/iː/	/ɛ/
breed	bred
feed	fed
sleep	slept
keep	kept
lead	led
leave	left
read	read

Work in pairs. Ask and answer choosing from the verbs above. Remember to stress the verb, not the pronoun.

A: Did he f<u>ée</u>d it?
B: Yes, he f<u>é</u>d it.

Close up

Let's practice /æ/. Remember to open your mouth to say *a* but say *é* instead. In fact, if you look at the /æ/ symbol, you'll see an *a* and an *e*.

Zoom in

207 Exercise 1: Repeat these phrases and short sentences with /æ/. This is a long sound.

sad fat man	Scratch my back.	Batman sang.
lack of ham	Pack your bag.	Chat with Dad.
mad black cat	The rat ran at last.	Sam can't be a bad man.

208 Exercise 2: Repeat these sentences with /æ/ in initial position.

The **a**mbitious **a**mbassador was **a**ngry with the **a**mateur **a**mbulance driver.
The **a**gile **a**nchorman h**a**d no **a**libi for the **a**ccident.

Take a look at the words with /æ/ in Exercises 1 and 2 and complete the rule:

/æ/ is usually spelled with the letter ______________ between ____________,
or in ______________ position followed by a ______________.

209 Exercise 3: Repeat these sentences with /æ/.

You c**a**n't c**a**tch s**al**mon in fl**a**t l**a**nd.
Adam c**a**n't st**a**nd d**a**ncing r**a**p.
P**a**m is gl**a**d her c**a**ttle are in the p**a**sture.
Don't l**au**gh at my **au**nt's pl**ai**d c**a**p.

Note: ***ant*** – always /ænt/
aunt – /ænt/ (mainly American) or /ɑnt/ (mainly British)

Exercise 4: Many irregular verbs with /ɪ/ make their past tense with /æ/.

ring /ɪ/ – rang /æ/

Can you think of any other verbs? Complete the table in pairs.

/ɪ/	/æ/

Also: run /ʌ/ – ran /æ/

Check the **Answer Key** before you do the next exercise.

210 Exercise 5: Complete the sentences using the verbs in Exercise 4.

Matt ___________ down, ___________ black rum and ___________ sadly.
Sam ___________ till his pants ___________.
Pam ___________ to chat with Nat in January.

Now listen, check your answers and repeat the sentences.

Conversation

211 Practice this conversation in pairs, paying attention to the /æ/ sound.

Sally: Pam, you can dance, can't you?
Pam: I'm no professional dancer, but I can jazz and tap. Why do you ask, Sally?
Sally: Jack asked me to a dance, and he's a fabulous dancer. In fact, I drag as a fat cat, and I'm so embarrassed. I can't go unless I look attractive. Pam, you have to give me a hand!
Pam: I'll teach you all I can, Sal. Then we'll buy you some eye-catching pants. OK?
Sally: Thanks, Pam. You're a real pal.

Close up

The most obvious way to differentiate /ɛ/ and /æ/ is to listen for the different sounds. Another way, though, is to look at the speaker's mouth to see what sound is being articulated: the speaker will open his or her mouth a lot wider to produce the /æ/ sound!

Get your tongue around it

212 Exercise 1: Repeat these pairs of words.

/ɛ/ (short)	/æ/ (long)
ten	tan
pen	pan
men	man
said	sad
bed	bad
send	sand

Work in pairs. Articulate one of the words above silently. Your friend will have to identify /æ/ or /ɛ/ just looking at your mouth and say “long” or “short.” Note that if you move your muscles correctly, and pay attention to duration, you don’t have to actually hear the sound to identify it.

213 Exercise 2: Listen to these groups of words.

1	2	3	4
/i:/	/ɪ/	/ɛ/	/æ/
beat	bit	bet	bat
bead	bid	bed	bad
meet	mitt	met	mat
deed	did	dead	dad
keen	kin	Ken	can

Now do the same activity silently, and try to guess which of the four sounds your friend is mouthing. Identify the sound by its number.

Stay tuned

214 Listen and circle the word you hear.

1. The *vet / vat* is in the barn.
2. The *pen / pan* is on the table.

3. I couldn't find *bread / Brad.*
4. My *celery / salary* is awful!
5. Where did you place the *bet / bat*?
6. This is what was really *said / sad.*
7. Try not to mix the *sexes / saxes.*
8. The *men / man* arrived.

Get your tongue around it

Work in pairs. Choose one of the possibilities in each question and ask a classmate. He/She has to listen up and give an appropriate free response that shows he/she has identified the sound.

Example: What do you use a pedal for?
paddle

A: What do you use a pedal for?
B: To make a bike go.
A: What do you use a paddle for?
B: To play racquetball.

1. Do you know why he left?
laughed?

2. Why do you need a pen?
pan?

3. Why did the man run?
men

4. Who's going to marry Ellen?
Alan?

5. Where's the wonderful gem?
jam?

Conversation

215 Repeat this conversation with /æ/ and /ɛ/.

Ted: Hi, Alan. Have you met Jack, the new manager?

Alan: I have, Ted. I guess Jack hasn't impressed you very well, has he?

Ted: Correct. He acts as if he's better than everyone else when we're by ourselves, and he pretends to be friendly when the general manager is present.

Alan: There's more. Jack asked Cathy, his secretary, to prepare his breakfast – eggs included – and yelled at her because she wasn't fast enough. Man, was Cathy mad!

Ted: Let's just say a prayer so Jack won't last!

/fə'nætɪk fər fə'nɛtiks/

Identify the words and write /ɛ/ or /æ/. Think of the spelling rules you have studied!

1. ch/___/nce
2. /___/lephant
3. chimp/___/nzee
4. h/___/ppen
5. w/___/ther
6. r/___/cipe
7. p/___/r
8. d/___/nce
9. b/___/nk
10. p/___/ragr/___/ph
11. h/___/vy
12. g /___/t tog/___/ther

Fun time

✎ In groups, complete the chart with words with /ɛ/ and /æ/. The first group to finish is the winner!

month	/ɛ/: ___ /æ/: ___	country	/ɛ/: ___ /æ/: ___
animal	/ɛ/: ___ /æ/: ___	part of the house	/ɛ/: ___ /æ/: ___
food	/ɛ/: ___ /æ/: ___	color	/ɛ/: ___ /æ/: ___
object	/ɛ/: ___ /æ/: ___	place around town	/ɛ/: ___ /æ/: ___

Wrap up

Go back to **Think about it** and go over the questions again. Then check your answers in the **Answer Key**.

Unit 3: /uː/ as in *blue* and /ʊ/ as in *book*

Think about it

✎ Say the word *blue*. Now say the word *book*. Are the "u" sounds different? Answer these questions.

1. Look at the illustration. What sound do the highlighted words in the question have in common? How about the words in the answer?
2. For which "u" sound are your lips more rounded?
3. For which "u" sound are your cheek muscles more relaxed?
4. Which "u" sound is longer?
5. Which "u" is more similar to the Portuguese "u?"

Don't look at the **Answer Key** now! Study the unit to the end and then check your answers.

Close up

Portuguese has only one “u” sound. English, however, has two: the long /u:/ and the short /ʊ/. The Portuguese “u” is similar to /u:/ in English, but not as long. When you pronounce /u:/, your lips are rounded and your cheek muscles are tense. When you pronounce /ʊ/, your lips are not so rounded and your cheek muscles are relaxed.

Zoom in

216 Exercise 1: Repeat these words with /u:/. Remember that this sound is **long and tense**, and your lips are rounded.

fl**ew** / fl**u**
d**o**
J**u**ne
s**ou**p
tr**ue**
s**oo**n
t**oo**th
cl**ue**
sh**oe**

Pay attention to these words pronounced with /u:/: *tomb* /tu:m/ and *super*

217 Exercise 2: Repeat these phrases with /u:/.

S**ue**’s b**oo**ts
ch**oo**se the fr**ui**t
s**u**per t**oo**l
z**oo** r**u**les
a bl**ue** s**ui**t
ch**ew** your f**oo**d
M**o**vie on T**ue**sday?
Wh**o** will l**o**se?

218 Exercise 3: When /u:/ is followed by /l/, sometimes you can hear a schwa sound /ə/ after the /u:/. Listen and repeat.

fool
pool
sch**ool**
st**ool**
cool
rule

219 Exercise 4: As we saw in Part B, Unit 8, many times /u:/ is preceded by /y/. Repeat the following words with /yu:/.

f**ew**	arg**ue**	**u**se
m**u**sic	vi**ew**	**u**niversity

Exercise 5: Complete these sentences with words with /u:/ or /yu:/.

1. Beth is in the living ________________.
2. *Old* is the opposite of ________________.
3. Think about the past, present and ________________.
4. Witches fly on ________________.
5. *A lot* is the opposite of *a* ________________.
6. One plus one equals ________________.
7. Strong shoes with tall tops are called ________________.
8. My favorite color is ________________.
9. You can swim in the ________________.
10. Don't lie. Tell me the ________________.

220 Listen and check your answers. Read the sentences in pairs. Then write two similar sentences and ask your classmates to complete them.

Get your tongue around it

Lou is surprised at the different things Prue does. Substitute the verbs as in the example.

do kung fu

Lou: *Pr**ue**, is it tr**ue** you do kung f**u**?*
Prue: *It's tr**ue**, L**ou**. I've been doing kung f**u** for over tw**o** years.*

ch**ew** a f**ew** r**oo**ts / **u**se a s**u**per sc**oo**ter / br**ew** pr**u**ne verm**ou**th / gr**ou**p tr**ou**pers to play sn**oo**ker / gl**ue** r**u**lers on your sh**oe**s

Zoom in

221 Exercise 1: Repeat these words with /ʊ/. Remember that this is a **short sound**. Don't round your lips.

Possible spellings:

oo	ou (modals)	CuC	others
good	should	put	woman
wood	would	bush	wolf
cook	could	sugar	
foot		butcher	
wool		full	

Pay attention to the pronunciation of /ʊ/ in the words *put*, *push*, *cushion* and *bush*, which are often mispronounced.

222 Exercise 2: Repeat these words with /ʊr/ and /yʊr/.

/ʊr/		/yʊr/	
poor	tour	cure	pure
sure	assure	curious	furious

The /ʊr/ is the words on the left can be pronounced /ɜr/ or /ɔr/ in some dialects.

223 Exercise 3: Repeat these sentences paying attention to the /ʊ/ sound.

Pull the hook from the pulley.
The wolf is by the bush.
The crook is putting on a hood.
The cook needs sugar to make cookies and pudding.

Get your tongue around it

The past tense of these verbs is pronounced with /ʊ/. Report these sentences as in the example.

"I take the bus every day."
He said he took the bus every day.

1. I shake the butcher's hand.
2. I put on a hood to avoid the soot.
3. I stand up to greet Brooke.
4. I can go to the brook on foot.
5. I will push the poor wolf.
6. I look good.
7. I understand the cookbook.

Zoom in

224 Exercise 1: Repeat these pairs of words.

/u:/ - /ʊ/	/u:/ - /ʊ/
pool – pull fool – full suit – soot Luke – look cooed – could	who'd – hood shoed – should wooed – wood/would stewed – stood

225 Exercise 2: All these words are spelled with "oo" but their pronunciation is different. There's no way to predict the sound. You just have to practice. Compare.

/u:/	/ʊ/
broom	took
spoon	stood
moon	wool
room	look
mood	wood
food	foot
choose /tʃu:z/	cook
goose /gu:s/	good

226 Exercise 3: Repeat these sentences with /u:/ and /ʊ/.

Brooke was in no mood to clean the room with a broom.
Woody looked at the good food Sue cooked.
Lou stood up and pushed the stool.
The cook always chooses the wooden spoon.
The wool boots are on the footstool.

Stay tuned

227 Listen, repeat and write /u:/ or /ʊ/. Remember: if you round your lips, it's /u:/.

1. good /ʊ/
2. lose ___
3. woman ___
4. human ___
5. crooked ___
6. furious ___
7. fuse ___
8. hook ___
9. student ___
10. tomb ___
11. butcher ___
12. wolf ___

In pairs, make sentences using the words above.

In context

228 Exercise 1: Practice the names of these books with /uː/ and /ʊ/.

On Food and Cooking, by Harold McGee
Feeling Good: the New Mood Therapy, by David D. Burns
Curious George Visits the Zoo, by Alan J. Shalleck
The True Woman: the Beauty and Strength of a Godly Woman, by Susan Hunt
Push and Pull (Rookie Read-About Science), by Patricia J. Murphy
A Conspiracy of Fools: A True Story, by Kurt Eichenwald
Fool Moon, by Jim Butcher
Wolf, by Becky Bloom
New York Dead, by Stuart Woods

229 Exercise 2: Listen to this conversation.

A: I'm looking for a book: Fool Moon, by Jim Butcher.
B: Sorry, but we should be receiving Fool Moon next Tuesday. Would you like to choose another book?
A: Well, do you have *Wolf* by Becky Bloom?
B: Here it is. Would you like me to put it in a blue box?
A: Yes, thanks. It looks good!

Exercise 3: Use the names of the books above to practice this conversation with a partner. Use some of the words in the box in the last two lines.

good – should – could – would – poor – sure – new – true – soon – super – school – cool

A: I'm looking for a book: ____________, by ____________.
B: Sorry, but we should be receiving ____________ next Tuesday. Would you like to choose another book?
A: Well, do you have ____________ by ____________?
B: ____?
A: ____.

/fə'nætɪk fər fə'nɛtɪks/

✎ Match the sentences and the transcriptions. There are two extra sentences!

1. The food the fool cooked made me full.
2. The food the fool cooked was good.
3. The fool understood the good book.
4. The full moon looked truly good.
5. The fool understood he could move the book.
6. The fool threw the food into the brook.

a. ( ) /ðə fu:d ðə fu:l kʊkt wəz gʊd/
b. ( ) /ðə fu:l ˌʌndər'stʊd ðə gʊd bʊk/
c. ( ) /ðə fʊl mu:n lʊkt 'tru:li gʊd /
d. ( ) /ðə fu:l θru: ðə fu:d 'ɪntʊ ðə brʊk/

Fun time

In pairs, answer these questions as truthfully as possible. Begin your answers with *If* ________.

What would you do if...
- you were a good cook?
- you wanted to look good?
- you met a wolf in the woods?
- a woman pushed you?
- you needed a new suit?
- a poodle pooed on your shoe?
- you never understood anything at school?
- a fool drooled on you?

Wrap up

Go back to **Think about it** and go over the questions again. Then check your answers in the **Answer Key**.

Unit 4: /ɑ/ as in *bar* and /ɔ/ as in *four*

Think about it

Discuss the following questions in pairs.

1. Are these statements true or false?

a. Words such as *hot dog* can be pronounced /ˈhɑt ˌdɑg/ or /ˈhɔt ˌdɔg/. ___
b. Most Americans say /ˈhɔt ˌdɔg/. ___
c. *Saw* in English and *só* in Portuguese sound the same. ___
d. Compare the word *bar* in English and in Portuguese. The /ɑ/ is longer in English. ___

2. Put the words in the correct column according to the sound of the letters in bold.

s**er**geant – t**a**lk – h**ear**t – c**a**ll – br**a** – l**aw** – c**a**lm – w**ar** – **au**thor – gu**ar**d

/ɑ/ as in *bar*	/ɔ/ as in *four*

Don't look at the **Answer Key** now! Study the unit to the end and then check your answers.

Close up

The sound /ɔ/ in English is similar to *ó* in Portuguese, but /ɔ/ is longer than ó, so *saw* and *só* do not sound exactly the same.

/ɔ/ has many possible spellings:

- *au* or *aw* as in *daughter* and *law*
- *a* followed by *l* or *ll* as in *always* and *mall*
- *o* followed by *ng* as in *wrong*
- *o* followed by *ff*, *th* or *ss* as in *off*, *moth* and *cross*
- *augh* or *ough* as in *caught* or *thought*

Important note: the words above can also be pronounced with /ɑ/ instead of /ɔ/. The words that are exclusively pronounced /ɔ/ are spelled as follows:

- o, *ou* or *oo* followed by *r* as in *or*, *four* and *door*

In some varieties of American English, words like *call* and *daughter* are pronounced with /ɑ/; likewise, in some places, words like *hot* and *cop* are pronounced with /ɔ/. Don't worry about having to change your pronunciation if you speak in the range of accuracy. Use this book as a guide to what is considered correct American English pronunciation, but be ready to hear – and understand – many variants.

Zoom in

230 Exercise 1: Listen to these words with /ɔ/.

auditorium	f**a**ll	l**o**ng	fl**oo**r	t**augh**t	c**o**ffee	acr**o**ss	w**a**r
awful	b**a**ld	wr**o**ng	p**ou**r	b**ough**t	**o**ffice	l**o**ss	w**a**rm
d**aw**n	w**a**lk	str**o**ng	st**o**re	f**ough**t	c**o**ffin	cl**o**th	w**a**rn

231 Exercise 2: Repeat these sentences.

The **Au**stralian h**o**rse has f**a**llen on the l**aw**n.
The **Au**strian **o**fficer had a l**o**ng t**a**lk with his d**augh**ter in **Au**gust.
The b**a**ld l**aw**yer **a**lways put his **au**dio books in the dr**aw**er.
The **au**dience didn't appl**au**d the **aw**ful **au**thor.
They th**ough**t they s**aw** D**o**ris y**aw**n.

Compare these pairs of words:

/ɔ/	/oʊ/	/ɔ/	/oʊ/
bald –	bold	cloth –	clothes

Conversation

232 Exercise 1: Listen to the conversation. Practice in pairs.

Cory: M**o**rning, L**au**ra. Your landl**o**rd c**a**lled at f**ou**r. He wanted to t**a**lk about the f**au**cet.
Laura: Finally! W**a**ter has been p**ou**ring **a**ll over my fl**oo**r. My d**augh**ter has f**a**llen and hit her f**o**rehead on the c**o**rner of the dr**aw**er.
Cory: That's app**a**lling! You must have f**ough**t with the landl**o**rd!
Laura: I w**a**rned him I would rep**o**rt him to the auth**o**rities. He looked b**o**red and returned to his ch**o**res. I was at a l**o**ss and just b**aw**led.
Cory: What a h**o**rrible st**o**ry!

Exercise 2: Answer these questions about the story with short answers. All the answers contain the /ɔ/ sound. Try not to look at the story!

1. Who called Laura?
2. What time did he call?
3. What did he want to talk about?
4. Who's Laura talking to?
5. What's pouring all over the floor?
6. Who has fallen?
7. Where has she hit her forehead?
8. Who did Laura want to report the landlord to?
9. How did the landlord look?
10. How did Cory describe the story?

Close up

In Portuguese when you are disappointed, you make the sound *Ah...* This corresponds to /ɑ/ in English, as /ɑ/ is longer than the regular "a" in Portuguese. It's usually spelled:

- o between consonants (C o C) or in stressed initial position, as in *pot* and *object*
- a followed by r (a + r), as in *start*

Many Brazilians pronounce words written C o C with the sounds /ɔ/, which is closer to the British standard pronunciation. You don't have to worry about changing your pronunciation. Just make sure you can recognize these words as an American will most probably pronounce them – with the sound /ɑ/.

Zoom in

233 Exercise 1: Repeat these phrases with /ɑ/ spelled *a* + *r*.

sharp and hard   a garden party   guard the park

Pay attention to the silent letters in these words:
Silent "u": g**u**ard /gɑrd/
Silent "l": ca**l**m /kɑm/ - ba**l**m /bɑm/ - pa**l**m /pɑm/

234 Exercise 2: Practice these words spelled C o C with "o" pronounced /ɑ/, as most Americans would say them. Repeat.

l**o**ck the b**o**x
sh**o**t the f**o**x
sh**o**pping for s**o**cks
on the d**o**t
b**o**dy cl**o**ck
odds and p**o**ssibilities
h**o**t **o**bject
g**o**t an **O**scar
p**o**cket **o**pera

235 Exercise 3: Here are some atypical spellings for /ɑ/. Listen and repeat.

f**a**ther
br**a**
faç**a**de
cors**a**ge
s**e**rgeant
h**ea**rt
entree
entrepreneur
ensemble

236 Exercise 4: Repeat these sentences with /ɑ/.

The word *gone* can be pronounced /gɑn/ or /gɔn/, and it doesn't rhyme with *done* /dʌn/.

Th**o**mas is a p**o**pular d**o**ctor in Chic**a**go.
Operator J**o**hn dis**a**rmed the cl**o**ck on the b**o**mb in the b**o**x.
My f**a**ther has g**o**ne to c**o**llege in Color**a**do.
The c**o**ps p**a**rked their c**a**r in H**a**rvard Y**a**rd.
H**o**nestly, B**o**b is a pr**o**blem t**o**ddler.
The sl**o**ppy r**o**ck st**a**r has a l**o**ft **o**n our bl**o**ck.

Stay tuned

237 Listen to this paragraph and fill in the blanks. All the words will have the sound /ɑ/.

Polly and Mark wanted to buy presents for their family, so they went to the shopping mall. Polly got a ________________ of ________________ for her father, but Mark just got ________________. Polly got some ______________ lotion for their mother, but Mark only got a cheap ________________. Polly got a Barbie ________________ for their little sister, but Mark only got a ________________ of chocolates. Polly got a toy ________________ for their little brother, but Mark only got him a pet ________________. Polly shouted at Mark, "________________! I'm ________________! What are you going to get me, then? A ________________?" Mark replied, "Right on the ________________!"

Repeat the paragraph.

In context

Do you know what star starred what movie? Match the columns.

1. ( ) Pierce Br**o**snan
2. ( ) Jane F**o**nda
3. ( ) T**o**m Hanks
4. ( ) T**o**m Cruise
5. ( ) Dustin H**o**ffman
6. ( ) J**o**hnny Depp
7. ( ) Julia R**o**berts

a. *Sleepy H**o**llow, Ch**a**rlie and the Ch**o**colate Factory*
b. *Erin Br**o**kovich, N**o**tting Hill, C**o**nspiracy Theory*
c. *T**o**p Gun, Mission Imp**o**ssible*
d. *You've G**o**t Mail*
e. ***O**n Golden P**o**nd, M**o**nster-in-Law*
f. *James B**o**nd – Tom**o**rrow Never Dies*
g. *C**o**nfidence, Meet the F**o**ckers*

Talk about these movie stars and movies.

A: Did Pierce Br**o**snan st**a**r in *Sleepy H**o**llow* and *Ch**a**rlie and the Ch**o**colate Factory*?

B: I'm n**o**t sure, but I think that was Johnny Depp.
A: Have you w**a**tched any other film st**a**rring Johnny Depp?
B: Yes, in fact... / No, but...

/fəˈnætɪk fər fəˈnɛtɪks/

Fill in the blanks with the words transcribed below.

/bɔt/	/wɔr/	/mɔl/
/blɑk/	/ˈkɑlərz/	/rɪˈkɔl/
/ˈprɑmɪst/	/ˈdɑlərz/	/sɔŋz/
/prɑm/	/rɑk/	/dʒɔrdʒ/

It was *prom* night, and all the seniors at St. ________ High School were very excited. There was going to be a ________ band, and they ________ to play all the most popular ________. Some of the girls spent thousands of ______ on their dresses, and boys ________ them the most beautiful corsages at the ________. All the boys ________ white ________ and ties and music could be heard all around the ________. It was a night they would ________ for the rest of their lives.

Fun time

Play *I went on a trip*. Use only words with /ɑ/ or /ɔ/. Follow the model.

A: I went on a trip and I took a doll with me.
All: I went on a trip and I took a doll with me.
B: I went on a trip and I took a doll and some coffee with me.
All: I went on a trip and I took a doll and some coffee with me.
C: I went on a trip and I took a doll and some coffee and ___ with me.
All: I went on a trip and I took a doll and some coffee and ___ with me.

Go on without repeating any words. If you fail to come up with a new word, you're out.

Wrap up

Go back to **Think about it** and go over the questions again. Then check your answers in the **Answer Key**.

Unit 5: /ʌ/ as in *but* and /ɜr/ as in *bird*

Think about it

Work on the questions below in pairs.

1. Do Brazilians have problems articulating /ʌ/ and /ɜr/?
2. What's the difference between /ʌ/ and /ə/?
3. What sound do these words have in common?

won – such – come – one – blood – rough

4. Place /ʌ/, /ɜr/ or /ə/ above the corresponding vowels. Each symbol is going to be used three times.

much   search   above   occur   curtain   son

Don't look at the **Answer Key** now! Study the unit to the end and then check your answers.

Close up

Some people refer to /ʌ/ as the stressed /ə/, and it's also known as the "Chinese hat" due to its shape. When this sound is followed by /r/, we use the symbol /ɜr/.

There's a lot of variation in relation to the phonetic notation of /ə/, /ʌ/ and /ɜr/. In order to simplify, some textbooks don't contrast these three sounds and use /ə/ for all three regardless of stress. However, most dictionaries do show this distinction.

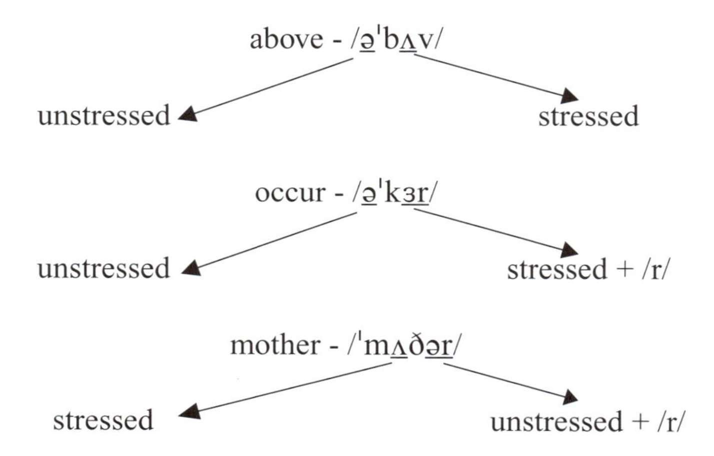

Brazilians in general have no trouble articulating /ʌ/ and /ɜr/. The only problem is mispronouncing words which sometimes are very common, and using another vowel sound instead.

Example:
/ʌ/
country - typical mistake: /aʊ/

/ɜr/
f**ir**m – typical mistake: /ɪr/

/ʌ/
pron**u**nciation - typical mistake: /aʊ/, because of the verb to

/aʊ/
pron**ou**nce

The problem is mispronunciation due to spelling, not articulation.

Also, be careful not to nasalize these sounds, especially when they are followed by nasals, /m, n, ŋ/. The Portuguese "*ã*" does not exist in English.

Zoom in

238 Exercise 1: Repeat these troublesome words with /ʌ/ and /ɜr/.

w**o**n	l**o**ve	ci**r**cle
tr**ou**ble	c**o**lor	w**or**k
c**ou**ntry	t**o**ngue	w**or**d
c**u**lture	br**o**ther	f**ir**m

Mr. Won wonder if someone won the sum of one hundred bucks.

Remember that *one* and *won* are homophones: /wʌn/!

Contrast the vowel sounds:

/ʌ/ /ɑ/
m**o**ther **but** f**a**ther

/ʌ/ /ɑ/
br**o**ther **but** b**o**ther

239 Exercise 2: Repeat these phrases and short sentences with /ʌ/ and /ɜr/.

m**o**ther t**o**ngue
s**o**me c**our**age
the **o**ther f**ir**m
one f**ir**st t**ur**n
My c**ou**ntry w**o**n.

C**o**me at **o**nce, j**er**k.
My c**o**mpany's in L**o**ndon.
S**ear**ch for the c**u**p.
There's j**u**st en**ou**gh bl**oo**d.
My br**o**ther's pron**u**nciation st**u**nk!

> Although the word *colonel* has no "r," it's pronounced just like the word *kernel*, /ˈkɜrnəl/.
> Ex: *Colonel Saunders created the recipe for KFC.*

240 Exercise 3: Repeat these sentences.

I h**ear**d the h**ur**t b**ir**d at the c**ir**cus.
Does a w**or**m have a t**o**ngue?
C**olo**nel B**ur**ns s**ear**ched for the h**ur**t ins**ur**gent.
B**er**t d**oe**sn't **ear**n m**u**ch m**o**ney.

Close up

The /ɜrl/ as in *girl* is hard for Brazilians because we don't have this /r/ + /l/ sequence in our language. Besides, some students think /r/ and /l/ have to be pronounced at the same time, which makes the sounds impossible to articulate!

Let's practice. Very slowly, say the word *girl*, pronouncing one sound at a time: *girrrr-l*. Make sure your tongue touches the alveolar region for /l/. Try again: *girrrr-l*. Now link:
gir‿l - girl.

World creates more problems because it has three consecutive consonants: /r/+/l/+/d/. Follow the same procedure. Practice pronouncing *world* saying one sound at a time: wor-l-d. Say it very slowly, until you can articulate all the sounds more easily: wor-l-d.

Zoom in

241 Exercise 1: Practice these words with /ɜrl/, saying one sound at a time.

pearl – **curl** – **earl** – tw**irl**

242 Exercise 2: Repeat these sentences.

The **earl**'s **girl**friend has swi**rl**ing **curl**s.
The wo**rld** twi**rl**s and twi**rl**s.
The **earl** gave the gi**rl** the biggest **pearl** in the wo**rld**.

Conversation

243 Exercise 1: Practice this conversation in pairs.

A: **Mother**, I **love** this **pearl** necklace.
B: **Girl**, don't you ask me to **purchase** you **one**. You're too **young** to wear **pearls**. Where in the **world** did you see **girls** with **curls** wearing **pearl** necklaces?
A: **Earl's girlfriend** got **pearls** for her **birthday**.
B: **Done** then. When you **turn thirty** like **Earl**'s **girlfriend**, you'll get your **pearls** too.

Exercise 2: Organize the words in bold according to the sound:

/ʌ/	/ɜr/	/ɜrl/

Zoom in

244 Listen to these questions.

1. Why on earth is it absurd to buy a fur skirt?
2. Do girls flirt with jerks and nerds?
3. What's worse: to be dumb or tough and rough?

4. Was your cousin your first love?
5. Do you prefer girls with curls or with brushed hair?

Now ask and answer the questions in pairs. Write two similar questions with /ʌ/, /ɜr/ and /ɜrl/ and ask your class.

Stay tuned

245 Exercise 1: Compare these pairs of words. Listen and repeat.

/ʌ/	/ʊ/
l**u**ck	l**oo**k
c**u**d	c**ou**ld
b**u**ck	b**oo**k
st**u**d	st**oo**d
t**u**ck	t**oo**k

246 Exercise 2: Listen and check the sentence you hear.

1. a. How many bucks do you want?
   b. How many books do you want?

2. a. They tuck him in.
   b. They took him in.

3. a. Did you say *stud*?
   b. Did you say *stood*?

4. a. My luck almost killed her.
   b. My look almost killed her.

5. a. How do you spell *cud*?
   b. How do you spell *could*?

Zoom in

247 Exercise 1: Compare these pairs of words. Listen and repeat.

/ʌ/	/ɑ/
n**u**t	n**o**t/kn**o**t
c**u**p	c**o**p
b**u**ddy	b**o**dy
c**o**lor	c**o**llar
d**u**ck	d**o**ck
f**u**nd	f**o**nd
b**u**m	b**o**mb

A b**u**m is a beggar who d**oe**sn't **ear**n m**o**ney by w**or**king.

248 Exercise 2: Identify the sounds in these sentences. Underline the sounds /ʌ/ and /ɜr/ and circle /ɑ/.

It’s hot in this country.
Lock the hut or trust your luck.
My puppy ate all the poppies in the garden.
My heart hurts.
There’s one buck in the box.
I heard about the hard work.
Don’t bother my brother, my father or my mother.

Now practice in pairs.

Stay tuned

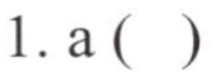 **249** Listen to these sentences and choose the correct pictures.

1. a ( )

1. b ( )

2. a ( )

2. b ( )

3. a ( )

3. b ( )

4. a ( )

4. b ( )

5. a ( )

5. b ( )

6. a ( )

6. b ( )

7. a ( )

7. b ( )

/fəˈnætɪk fər fəˈnɛtiks/

Write the transcribed minimal pairs:

/fæn/	*fan*	/hɑt/	
/fɪn/	*fin*	/hæt/	
/fʌn/	*fun*	/hʌt/	
		/hɜrt/	
/lɑk/		/hɑrt/	
/lʊk/			
/læk/		/bɑks/	
/lʌk/		/bʊks/	
/li:k/		/bʌks/	
/fɜrm/		/bɜrd/	
/fɑrm/		/bɔrd/	
/fɔrm/		/bɪrd/	

Fun time

Play Battleship with a friend. Draw in your ships vertically and horizontally according to the list below.

one ship that is 3 squares long
three ships that are 2 squares long
two ships that are 1 square long

You have to find all of your opponent's ships. If the opponent hits a ship of yours, you have to say, "Hit!" If there are no ships on the square, you say, "Miss!" Once a whole ship has been hit, the person losing it must say, "Sunk!" At the end of the game compare your sheets to see if there were any mistakes. The trick here is that instead of the traditional letters and numbers you have words with different vowel sounds. Pronouncing the words incorrectly or not understanding them might cost you a battle!

Follow the example:

A: Stock – neat
B: Miss! Body – stir
A: Hit!

US

	store	stir	knit	neat	stick	buddy	cot
star							
not							
nut							
stock							
stuck							
cut							
body							

THEM

	store	stir	knit	neat	stick	buddy	cot
star							
not							
nut							
stock							
stuck							
cut							
body							

Wrap up

Go back to **Think about it** and go over the questions again. Then check your answers in the **Answer Key**.

Unit 6: /eɪ/ as in *pay* and /oʊ/ as in *go*

Think about it

Discuss these questions.

1. Why do English speakers say things like "beibei" instead of "bebê" and "coucou" instead of "coco" when they are learning Portuguese?

2. Can a final silent letter "e" (such as in *mak<u>e</u>* or *not<u>e</u>*) help you guess the pronunciation of a word?

3. Pronounce these words. Separate the words in two groups according to the sound of the underlined vowel.

though
danger
bowl
sole
bracelet
toe
Joan
steak
valet
sew
main
freight
obey

/eɪ/	/oʊ/

Don't look at the **Answer Key** now! Study the unit to the end and then check your answers.

Close up

In Portuguese, /e/ and /o/ are pure sounds. In English, however, these sounds never occur by themselves: they always come as /eɪ/ and /oʊ/. These double sounds are called glides. Compare:

Portuguese	English
Roma	R**o**me /oʊ/
omite	**o**mit /oʊ/
filé	fil**et** /eɪ/
balê	ball**et** /eɪ/

Zoom in

250 Exercise 1: Repeat these phrases with /eɪ/.

s**a**m**e** dom**ai**n | pl**ay** the g**a**m**e** | w**ai**t at the g**a**t**e**
b**a**k**e** a c**a**k**e** | st**ay** aw**ay** | m**a**d**e** in Sp**ai**n

251 Exercise 2: Repeat these words with /eɪn/. Make sure your tongue touches the alveolar ridge for /n/.

r**ain** – expl**ain** – ch**an**ge – d**an**ger – m**ain** – s**ain**t – f**ain**t

> Remember *My Fair Lady?*
> *The rain in Spain stays mainly in the plain!*

Look at the words in Exercises 1 and 2 and complete the spelling rule.

The sound /eɪ/ is usually spelled:

a. ___ or ___
b. C ___ C + silent ___

252 Exercise 3: These words are pronounced with /eɪ/. Notice the unusual spelling.

br**ea**k – st**ea**k – gr**ea**t
eight – fr**eigh**t
ball**et** – val**et** – gourm**et***

Contrast:

/eɪ/	/ɛ/
br**ea**k	br**ea**kfast

253 Exercise 4: Repeat these sentences with /eɪ/:

I'm afr**ai**d the st**ea**k is not gr**ea**t.
L**a**ce Gr**ay** esc**a**ped from the st**a**te j**ai**l.
This s**a**cred pl**a**ce is the cr**a**dle of an **a**ncient civiliz**a**tion.
M**a**ke the m**ai**d ch**a**nge the br**a**celets.
The fr**eigh**t tr**ai**n from Sp**ai**n was del**ay**ed **eigh**t d**ay**s.

254 Exercise 5: Let's practice /oʊ/. Repeat these sentences.

Joe st**o**le the fl**oa**ting b**oa**t out in the **o**pen.
The c**o**ld sn**ow** fr**o**ze our b**o**nes.
Joan r**o**de the n**o**table c**o**lt in Oct**o**ber.
My f**o**lks d**o**n't like y**o**lk.

The "l" is silent in *fo̶lk* and *yo̶lk*!

255 Exercise 6: Pay special attention to the words with /oʊ/ followed by /l/. Make sure you pronounce the /l/! Your tongue touches the alveolar ridge.

toll – **bowl** – **coal** – **fold** – **gold** – **bold**

* French words

256 Exercise 7: The spelling of /oʊ/ is unusual in the following words:

toe – **foe** – **Joe**
th**ough** – alth**ough** – d**ough**nut
s**ew** – c**o**mb

In most British dictionaries, the notation for /oʊ/ is /əʊ/.

In context

Do you believe in these old wives' tales and superstitions? Discuss them in pairs.

1. You'll catch a c**o**ld if you str**o**ll around in the r**ai**n.
2. If your n**o**se itches, you'll have to h**o**st a guest.
3. There's g**o**ld at the end of the r**ai**nb**ow**.
4. It's bad luck to **o**pen an umbrella and h**o**ld it **o**ver your head inside the house.
5. Mang**o** and milk are a f**a**tal combin**a**tion.
6. All wind**ow**s should be **o**pened at the m**o**ment of death s**o** that the s**ou**l can g**o** aw**ay**.

Zoom in

257 Exercise 1: When "a" is between consonants followed by a silent "e," the "a" is pronounced /eɪ/. Compare:

C a C = /æ/	C a C + silent e = /eɪ/
fat	fate
snack	snake
mad	made
nap	nape
cat	Kate
cap	cape

258 Exercise 2: When "o" is between consonants followed by a silent "e," the "o" is pronounced /oʊ/. Compare:

C o C = /ɑ/	C o C + silent e = /oʊ/
rod	rode
cod	code
not	note
con	cone
pop	Pope

Notice the pronunciation of these words:
/oʊ/ /ɑ/ or /ɔ/
kn**ow** – kn**ow**ledge

Close up

The ***silent e rule*** is very useful to help you predict the pronunciation of many words. According to this rule, the silent e indicates that the previous vowel is pronounced as the name of the letter.

For example: dat*e* → silent ***e***

this letter is pronounced /eɪ/ so we say /deɪt/

name of the letters	
a – /eɪ/	m*a*ke /meɪk/
e – /i:/	sc*e*ne /si:n/
i – /aɪ/	l*i*ke /laɪk/
o – /oʊ/	b*o*ne /boʊn/
u – /yu:/	*u*se /yu:z/

There are exceptions, of course:

/ɪ/: live – give – since /ʌ/: come – done – some – love /ɑ/ or /ɔ/: gone

Also, notice what happens when the consonant doubles:

/aɪ/	/ɪ/
ride	ridden
write	written
bite	bitten
hide	hidden
diner	dinner

Even though we don't double the consonant in *driven*, it's also pronounced with /ɪ/!

A ***final "y"*** affects the previous vowel the same way as the silent e. However, it is pronounced /i/ and counts as a syllable.

/eɪ/ - l**a**zy, n**a**vy, b**a**by, l**a**dy, cr**a**zy
/oʊ/ - n**o**sy, c**o**zy, p**o**ny, T**o**ny, r**o**sy

Stay tuned

259 Exercise 1: Compare these pairs of words.

/ɛn/	/eɪn/	/æm/	/eɪm/
s**e**nt/c**e**nt/sc**e**nt	s**ai**nt	**a**m	**ai**m
m**e**n	m**ai**n	cl**a**m	cl**ai**m
tr**e**nd	tr**ai**ned	S**a**m	s**a**me
pl**a**n	pl**a**ne/pl**ai**n	l**a**mb	l**a**me

260 Exercise 2: Now compare these words with and without /l/.

/oʊ/	/oʊl/
tow/toe	**toll**
boat	**bolt**
towed/toad	**told**
sow/so/sew	**soul /sole**
bow	**bowl**
code	**cold**

261 Exercise 3: This is a dictation. Listen and write the words you hear.

1. ____________________
2. ____________________
3. ____________________
4. ____________________
5. ____________________
6. ____________________
7. ____________________
8. ____________________
9. ____________________
10. ____________________

Get your tongue around it

262 Repeat these sentences. Make sure you pronounce the /l/'s, /n/'s and /m/'s!

They st**ole** the g**ol**den gr**ain** from the **old** tr**ain**.
The f**oam** went down the d**an**gerous dr**ain**.
The c**ol**d r**ain** made them ch**an**ge pl**an**es in Stockh**ol**m.
The **aim** of the g**ame** is to hit the h**ole** by the p**ole**.

In context

Exercise 1: Read these questions.

1. What makes you go ape?
2. Do you think the man should always be the one to bring home the bacon?
3. Do you sometimes go against your grain to get something you want?

4. What do you think about people who lie to save face?
5. Are you the kind of person who makes a decision and always has a change of heart?
6. What job do you consider a gravy train?
7. Are you salting away to buy something important?
8. What is something you want to get that you wouldn't mind paying through the nose for?

Exercise 2: Match the idioms with /eɪ/ and /oʊ/ and their meanings.

A: What does *go ape* mean?
B: It means *behave in a crazy way*.

1. ( ) go ape / go bananas
2. ( ) bring home the bacon
3. ( ) go against the grain
4. ( ) save face
5. ( ) have a change of heart
6. ( ) gravy train
7. ( ) salt away
8. ( ) pay through the nose

a. pay a high price
b. work that pays more than it's worth
c. save your reputation
d. behave in a crazy way
e. save money
f. support the family
g. change your mind
h. go against your natural behavior

Now discuss the questions in pairs.

Conversation

263 Practice this conversation in pairs, paying attention to /eɪ/ and /oʊ/.

Moe: Jane, the plane is late, so why don't we take the train to Maine?
Jane: No, Moe, don't go over this. I won't go on the railroad.
Moe: Let's change trains on the way and we'll get to Maine at eight.
Jane: Are you afraid of planes or still stuck in the old travel modes? Go! The line is in motion!
Moe: Too late to run away! Let's just pray we'll be safe!

/fəˈnætɪk fər fəˈnɛtɪks/

Work in small groups. Look at the pictures and find words that rhyme. They are all one-syllable words. Then write the pairs of words under the corresponding vowel sound. The first group to finish correctly wins the game!

/ʌ/	/ɜr/	/ɑ/	/ɔ/
/ɛ/	/æ/	/i:/	/ɪ/
/eɪ/	/oʊ/	/u:/	/ʊ/
	note		
	boat		

Fun time

✎ Work in pairs. Match the rhyming words. There are three matches for each item. The first pair to do it correctly wins.

Set 1

1. ( )( )( ) done
2. ( )( )( ) gone
3. ( )( )( ) cone

a. won
b. own
c. Sean
d. ton
e. loan
f. prawn
g. sun
h. Bonn
i. sewn

Set 2

1. ( )( )( ) comb
2. ( )( )( ) bomb
3. ( )( )( ) tomb

a. balm
b. foam
c. broom
d. Tom
e. doom
f. Rome
g. palm
h. gnome
i. consume

Wrap up

Go back to **Think about it** and go over the questions again. Then check your answers in the **Answer Key**.

Unit 7: /aɪ/ as in *my*, /aʊ/ as in *cow* and /ɔɪ/ as in *boy*

Think about it

Do these activities in pairs.

1. Match the sounds with their usual spellings.

1. /aɪ/
2. /aʊ/
3. /ɔɪ/

a. ( ) oy ____________
b. ( ) ou ____________
c. ( ) ie ____________
d. ( ) C i C + silent e ____________
e. ( ) oi ____________
f. ( ) igh ____________
g. ( ) ow ____________
h. ( ) y ____________

2. Write a word as an example next to each spelling above.

3. /eɪ/ and /oʊ/ are called glides, while /aɪ/, /aʊ/ and /ɔɪ/ are called diphthongs. What's the difference between a glide and a diphthong if both are compound of two sounds?

Don't look at the **Answer Key** now! Study the unit to the end and then check your answers.

Close up

The difference between glides and diphthongs can be explained in two ways:

- A glide is a vowel accompanied by an adjacent sound. A diphthong is a vowel accompanied by a non-adjacent sound. Look at the chart to see how it goes:

glides: /eɪ/ – /oʊ/

/i:/ /ɪ/		/u:/ /ʊ/
/eɪ/ /ɛ/	/ʌ/ /ɛ/	/oʊ/
/æ/	/ɑ/	/ɔ/

diphthongs: /aɪ/ – /aʊ/ – /ɔɪ/

/i:/ /ɪ/		/u:/ /ʊ/
/eɪ/ /ɛ/	/ʌ/	/oʊ/
/æ/	/ɑ/	/ɔ/

- Other phoneticians call the attention to the fact that the sounds involved in the diphthongs occur by themselves: /ɑ/, /ɪ/, /ɔ/ and /ʊ/. Differently, the sounds involved in the glides are never pure vowels. The sounds /e/ and /o/ don't occur by themselves in English, appearing only in the glides /eɪ/ or /oʊ/.

Zoom in

264 Exercise 1: Repeat these words with /aʊ/.

ou	***ow***
cloud	clown
out	town
mouse	cow
found	renowned

265 Exercise 2: Repeat these words with /ɔɪ/.

oi	*oy*
ch**oi**ce	**oy**ster
b**oi**l	ann**oy**
c**oi**n	t**oy**

266 Exercise 3: Repeat these words with /aɪ/.

ie	*igh*	*y*
p**ie**	n**igh**t	m**y**
d**ie** / d**ye**	m**igh**t	cr**y**
t**ie**	h**igh**	terrif**y**
l**ie**	s**igh**	den**y**

These *–ing* forms are also pronounced /aɪ/.
Notice that *–ing* makes another syllable.

die – dying /ˈdaɪ-ɪŋ/
lie – lying /ˈlaɪ-ɪŋ/
tie – tying /ˈtaɪ-ɪŋ/

267 Exercise 4: Repeat these contrasting words. All the words in the second column have a *silent e*.

C i C = /ɪ/	C i C + silent e = /aɪ/ C y C + silent e = /aɪ/
bit	bite / byte
fin	fine
sit	site
dim	dime
win	wine
tip	type
still	style
rim	rhyme

268 Exercise 5: Repeat these words with atypical spelling of /aɪ/.

al**i**gn – s**i**gn – cl**i**mb
b**i**nd – m**i**nd – m**i**ld – w**i**ld
eye – d**ye** – r**ye**
g**uy** – b**uy**
h**ei**ght

Pay attention to the different vowel sounds:

/aɪ/ /ɪ/ /ɪ/
s**i**gn – s**i**gnature – s**i**gnal

/aɪ/ /ɪ/
w**i**ld – w**i**lderness

269 Exercise 6: Pay attention to the changes in these words related to measurements:

	adjective	noun
	h**igh** /aɪ/	h**eigh**t /aɪ/
	w**i**de /aɪ/	w**i**dth /ɪ/
	d**ee**p /iː/	d**e**pth /ɛ/
	l**o**ng /ɔ/	l**e**ngth /ɛ/
Also:	str**o**ng /ɔ/	str**e**ngth/ɛ/

270 Exercise 7: Repeat these sentences with:

/aʊ/: The br**ow**n m**ou**se and the c**ow** were not all**ow**ed in the t**ow**n h**ou**se.
/ɔy/: The j**oy**ful b**oy**s sp**oi**led their v**oi**ces at the n**oi**sy j**oi**nt.
/aɪ/: G**uy** the Kn**igh**t m**igh**t f**igh**t for his l**i**fe with his **i**vory kn**i**fe.

Zoom in

Exercise 1: Pay attention to these homographs.

/ɪ/	/aɪ/
live (v.)	live (adj.)
wind (n.)	wind (v.)

/u:/	/aʊ/
wound (n. or v.)	wound (past form)

/oʊ/	/aʊ/
bow (n.)	bow (v.)

✎ Exercise 2: Match the definitions or pictures to the transcriptions.

1. ___ /lɪv/
2. ___ /laɪv/
3. ___ /wɪnd/
4. ___ /waɪnd/
5. ___ /wu:nd/
6. ___ /waʊnd/
7. ___ /boʊ/
8. ___ /baʊ/

a. the natural movement of air

b. 

c. past of wind

d. 

e. broadcast at the time of the performance

f. 

g. to reside

h. 

Exercise 3: Look at the table on page 231 and write the correct symbol.

1. /___/ 2. /___/ 3. /___/
The show "Live and Let Live" is going on live tonight.

4 ./___/ 5. /___/
Rewind *Gone with the Wind*, please.

6. /___/ 7. /___/
The child got a wound as she wound the toy.

8. /___/ 9. /___/
He might die on the windy winding road.

10. /___/ 11. /___/
He bowed after he undid the bow.

271 Read the sentences in pairs to check your answers. Then listen to the model.

Get your tongue around it

272 Exercise 1: Listen to these *nouns and adjectives*. Change them into *verbs* by adding the suffix –ize /aɪz/. The stress remains in the same syllable as in the base word. Follow the model.

Model: *térror*
You: *térrorize*
Model: *térrorize*
You: *térrorize* (repetition)

273 Exercise 2: Change the *nouns and adjectives* you hear into *verbs* adding the suffix –ify /ɪfaɪ/.

Model: *púre*
You: *púrify*
Model: *púrify*
You: *púrify* (repetition)

✎ 274 Exercise 3: Now change the *nouns* ending in the suffix –ation into *verbs* by changing the suffix to –ify. Notice the **change in stress**.

Model: *identifi**cá**tion*
You: *i**dén**tify*
Model: *idéntify*
You: *idéntify* (repetition)

Conversation

275 Listen to this conversation.

Joyce: Roy's so joyful about his birthday, but I don't want to toil around a party with noisy boys.
Clyde: Instead, you can buy him a nice white Thai kite, or hire a guide to take him on a night bike ride. That's wild!
Howie: No doubt he'll prefer to go around with his crowd on his brown mountain bike.

Read the conversation in groups of three.

Stay tuned

✎ 276 Exercise 1: Listen and fill in the blanks with one of the words in parentheses. The spelling rules should help you do it correctly.

1. The hairdresser ____________________ my hair. (did / dyed)
2. At what time is our ____________________ arriving? (dinner / diner)
3. The secretary ____________________ the form. (filled / filed)
4. Those ____________________ look awful! (strips / stripes)

5. Susan is a ____________________ lady. (prim / prime)
6. This ____________________ is not working. (kit / kite)
7. I like the beautiful ____________________. (rim / rhyme)

Exercise 2: Now work in pairs. Read the sentences choosing one of the alternatives. Your partner has to make a free comment to show he understood what you said.

Example:

A: I like the beautiful rhyme.
B: Yeah, it sounds really great.

A: I like the beautiful rim.
B: You mean the rim of the hat?

Fun time

✎ Read the cue and think of the one-syllable word that would best complete it. All the answers contain a diphthong.

/aɪ/	-	/aʊ/	-	/ɔɪ/
1		2		3

Write the number corresponding to the diphthong. The first group to finish numbering the sentences correctly is the winner.

Example:

Milk is produced by (2). (The word *cows* has the sound /aʊ/.)

a. (   ) is a dark color.
b. That's not a girl, that's a (   ).
c. If I sell, you (   ).
d. Children play with (   ).
e. I bought it, so now it's (   ).

f. A small city is called a ( ).
g. Sing! I want to hear your ( ).
h. Stay here by my ( ).
i. Quiet! Don't make ( ).
j. A lot of people is a ( ).
k. It's not wrong, it's ( ).
l. It's not day, it's ( ).
m. ( ) plus ( ) equals fourteen.
n. Speak softly; don't ( ).
o. *At this moment* is the same as ( ).
p. I chose it. It was my ( ).
q. At 100° water will ( ).
r. A small rat is a ( ).
s. A *sofa* is also called a ( ).

/fəˈnætɪk fər fəˈnɛtɪks/

✎ This is the big challenge! Complete the crossword puzzle using phonetic symbols.

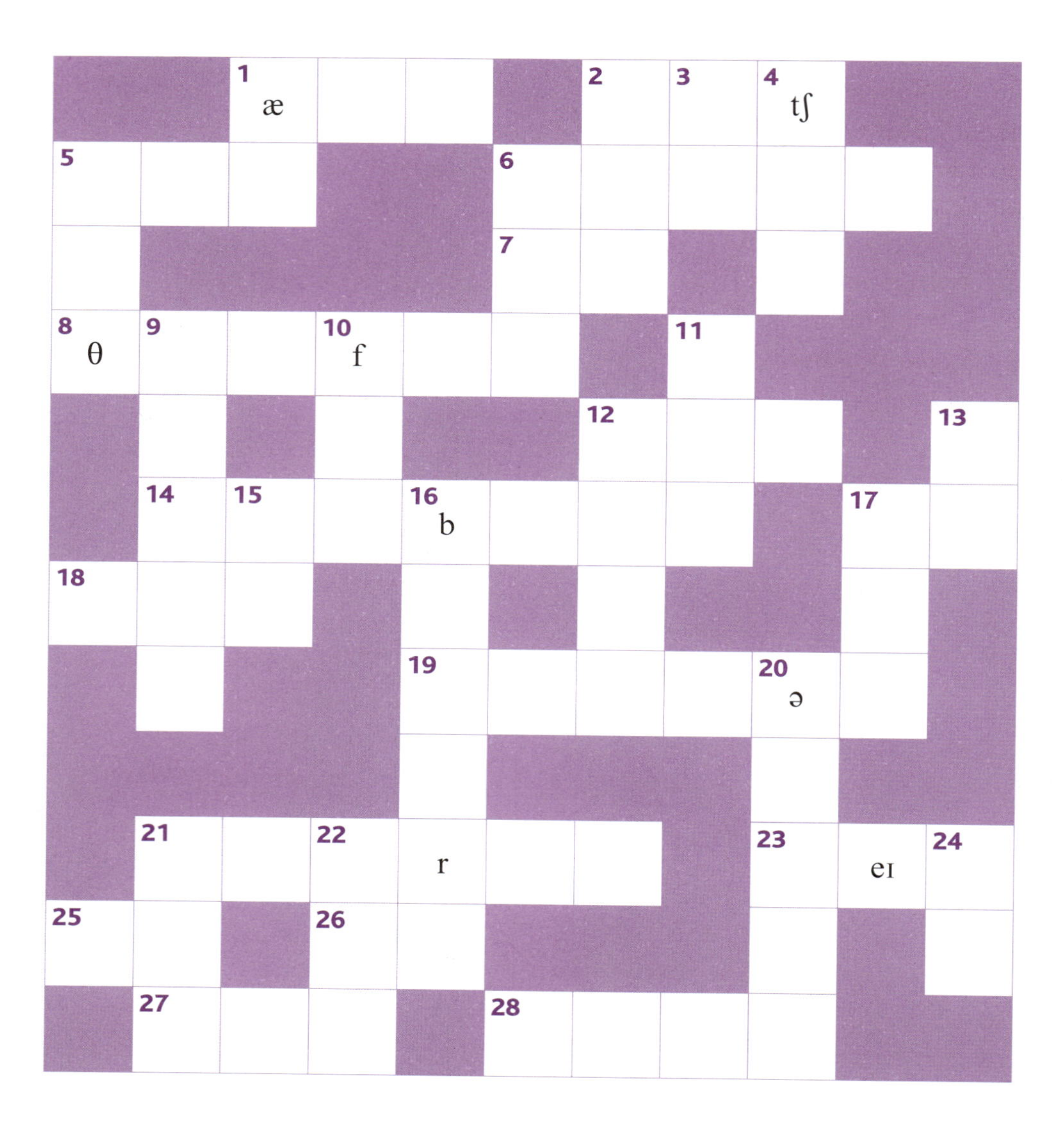

Across

1. You use it to cut wood.
2. get
5. red vegetable
6. not going
7. should = ________ to
8. thinking, caring
12. cut into pieces
14. advertise on the ________.
17. although
18. an alcoholic drink
19. cocoa
21. cold and good
23. a car _______
25. sick
26. Please be at _____.
27. a place for animals (pl.)
28. opportunity

Down

1. preposition
2. separate (v.)
3. I ________; you are
4. under your mouth
5. shower or ___
6. Give me a _____!
9. The planets ___ around the sun.
10. _____up the tank.
11. You sleep on it.
12. American for lorry
13. *Friends* is a TV ________.
15. You hear with your ________.
16. They sell meat.
17. not this
20. *address* pronounced as a verb
21. passages
22. You need these to open doors.
24. a kind of bean

Wrap up

Go back to **Think about it** and go over the questions again. Then check your answers in the **Answer Key**

Glossary of Technical Terms

accent
The particular way a person speaks, which tells you something about their background, like where they are from or their social level.

affricate
The sounds /tʃ/ and /dʒ/, which begin with a stop and continue with a *fricative*.

alveolar
Sounds produced with the tip of the tongue touching or approximating the tooth ridge, the area right behind the upper front teeth (/s/, /z/, /n/, /t/, /d/ and /l/).

articulation
The movements involved in the production of speech sounds in the vocal tract.

aspiration
Puff of air which accompanies the production of sounds like /p/, /t/, and /k/.

assimilation
A new sound that results from or facilitates the transition from the sound at the end of a word to the sound beginning another.

bilabial
Sound produced by the lips brought together: /p/, /b/, /m/ and /w/.

consonant sound
Sound produced by the partial or complete approximation (also known as obstruction) of articulators (tongue, palate, tooth, etc).

dental
Sound produced with the tongue tip on or near the inner surface of the upper teeth (/ð/, /θ/).

diagonal bars / /

Used to distinguish sounds from letters. For example, the letter "p" from the sound /p/.

dialect

A linguistic variety of a language which shows some difference from the variety considered "the standard." This variation could be in terms of vocabulary, pronunciation, or grammar.

diphthong

One sound made up of two vowels (/aɪ/, /ɔɪ/, /aʊ/).

flap

"t" or "d" in unstressed intervocalic position or preceded by /r/ and followed by a vowel sound (bu**tt**er, par**t**y, la**d**y).

fricative

Sound in which the air stream is forced through a narrow opening with resulting friction (/s/, /z/, /f/, /v/, etc).

glide

Sound produced when the mouth "glides" (moves) from one position to another (/eɪ/, /oʊ/).

glottal

Sound made in the larynx, through the narrowing of the glottis.

glottis

Space between the vocal folds (cords).

homographs

Two words that are spelled the same but sound different, like *tear* /tɪr/ and *tear* /tɛr/.

homophones

Two words that sound the same, but are spelled differently, like *meet* and *meat*.

intonation
The "musicality" or melody of a language.

IPA
International Phonetic Alphabet. A convention created by linguists to try to represent the sounds of any language in the world by means of the same graphic system.

labiodental
Sound produced when the upper teeth touch the lower lip (/f/ and /v/).

larynx
The Adam's apple; part of the respiratory tract where the vocal folds are located. It's between the pharynx and the trachea.

lateral
Sound produced with the tip of the tongue touching the alveolar ridge and the air escaping around the sides of the mouth (/l/).

linking
The connecting of the final sound of a word or syllable to the initial sound of the next, usually C+V.

liquid
The sounds /l/ and /r/.

minimal pair
Two words that sound the same except for one sound, like *get* / *bet* and *heard* / *hurt*.

morphology
The part of linguistics that studies the morphemes (smallest distinctive units of grammar) and how they combine to form words.

nasal
Sound produced with air escaping through the nose (/m/, /n/, /ŋ/).

native speaker
A person whose first language is the language in question. For example, a person who is born in Brazil is a native speaker of Portuguese.

organs of speech
The parts of the body that are used in the speech act: lungs, trachea, larynx and mouth.

palatal
Sound produced with the tongue approximating the palate (/ʃ/, /ʒ/).

palate
The roof of the mouth.

pharynx
The tube that goes from the back of the mouth to the separate passages for food (esophagus) and air (larynx).

phonetic alphabet
A set of phonetic symbols chosen to represent the sounds of a language.

phonetic symbol
The representation of the sound of a language.

phonetic transcription
The writing of the sound of a word in phonetic symbols.

phonology
The study of the sounds of a language.

plosive
Sound produced with complete obstruction of the air stream followed by a sudden release of air (/p/, /t/, /k/, /b/, /d/ and /g/).

retroflex
Sound made with the tip of the tongue curled back in the direction of the hard palate (/r/).

segmental
Segmental units are vowel and consonant sounds.

semivowels
Consonants that lack the articulatory features of consonants like closure or approximation of articulators; instead, they have the features common to vowels, like free passage of air. (/w/ and /y/)

sibilants
The s-like sounds, like /s/, /z/, /ʃ/, /ʒ/, /tʃ/ and /dʒ/.

silent "e"
The unpronounced letter "e" at the end of words. (lat***e***, lik***e***, cut***e***)

silent "e" rule
When we have the combination consonant + vowel + consonant + silent e, the vowel is usually pronounced according to its alphabetical value. For example:

gate – a = /eɪ/ coke – o = /oʊ/
dime – i = /aɪ/ tune – u = /yu:/

silent letters
Letters that are spelled but not pronounced in a word, like the *h* in *hour* or the *w* in *write*.

soft palate
See velum.

stop
See plosive.

stressed syllable
The syllable in a word that stands out and is more clearly pronounced.

suprasegmental features
Stress, rhythm and intonation.

syllabification
The separation of syllables.

trachea
Part of the respiratory tract between the larynx and the lungs, also called windpipe.

variety of English
The politically correct term for dialect.

VD
Voiced.

velar
A sound made with the back of the tongue against the soft palate or velum.

velum
The back of the roof of the mouth; the soft palate.

VL
Voiceless.

vocal folds/cords
The vibrating bands of tissue within the larynx.

voiced
Sound produced with the vibration of the vocal folds. Most consonants and all the vowels are voiced.

voiceless
Sound produced without the vibration of the vocal folds. They are: /p/, /t/, /k/, /s/, /f/, /θ/, /ʃ/ and /tʃ/.

vowel sound
Sound produced when the air comes out through the mouth freely, without approximation of the articulators.

Answer Key and Audio Scripts

Part A

Unit 1

Zoom in p.26

Exercise 1:

(3) go /oʊ/
(6) cup /ʌp/
(2) true /u:/
(1) cow /aʊ/
(7) cuff /ʌf/
(5) off /ɔf/
(4) caught /ɔ/

What's your conclusion? The same letters *ough* can have seven different pronunciations. We don't have anything like that in Portuguese, do we?

Exercise 2:

Portuguese			English		
word	letters	sounds	word	letters	sounds
bola	4	4	ball	4	3
imagine	7	7	imagine	7	6
chocolate	9	8	chocolate	9	6/7[2]
diferente	9	9	different	9	7/8[3]
ai	2	1	eye	3	1
fixa	4	5	ax	2	3
Lívia	5	5	leave	5	3
arrastar	8	7/6[1]	thought	7	3

1. 6 if you omit the final /r/.
2. chocolate – /ˈtʃɑkələt/ or /ˈtʃɑklət/
3. different – /ˈdɪfərənt/ or /ˈdɪfrənt/

What's your conclusion? In Portuguese the number of letters and sounds coincides more than in English.

Exercise 3:

(These are some examples. There are lots more.)

ea tea	ie believe	i ski
ee meet	ei receive	eo people
ey key	e me	oe phoenix

Unit 2

Zoom in p.30

Exercise 1:

stress (1)	smile (1)	rhythm (2)
airplanes (2)	through (1)	separate (adj.) (2/3*)
like (1)	missed (1)	separate (verb.) (3)
Portuguese (3)	police (2)	advertisement (4)

* separate = /ˈsɛpərət/ or /ˈsɛprət/

Exercise 5:

progress (n.)	politics	catholic
progress (v.)	political	contribute
democracy	politician	creative
independence	ignorance	develop

Unit 3

Zoom in p.36

(5) – (10) – (11) – (7) – (3) – (1) – (6) – (9) – (8) – (2) – (4) –
(3) – (8) – (4) – (11) – (2) – (7) – (6) – (1) – (10) – (5) – (9)

Zoom in p.39

Exercise 1:

/i:/	/ɪ/	/eɪ/	/ɛ/	/æ/	/ɑ/	/ʌ/	/ə/
zero three	six	eight	seven ten			one	seven

/ɜr/	/ɔ/	/oʊ/	/ʊ/	/u:/	/aɪ/	/aʊ/	/ɔɪ/
	four	*zero*		two	five nine		

Exercise 2:

gr / i:/ n
bl /æ/ ck
bl /u:/
p /ɪ/ nk
s /ɪ/ lv /ə/ r

wh /aɪ/ te
y /ɛ/ ll /oʊ/
br /aʊ/ n
b /eɪ/ ge

r /ɛ/ d
p /ɜr/ p /ə/ l
g /oʊ/ ld
gr /eɪ/

/fəˈnætɪk fər fəˈnɛtɪks/ p.39

1. tiger
2. cow
3. cat
4. bird
5. turkey
6. fish
7. chicken
8. elephant
9. zebra
10. camel
11. monkey
12. chimpanzee
13. sheep
14. rabbit
15. lion
16. crocodile
17. alligator
18. giraffe

Fun time p.40

a.11; **b.**8; **c.**5; **d.**16; **e.**12; **f.**9; **g.**3; **h.**13; **i.**15; **j.**6; **k.**1; **l.**10; **m.**4; **n.**2; **o.**7; **p.**14

Unit 4

Think about it p.41

1. All the pronunciations are correct.
2. a. flower / flour
   b. write / right
   c. sail / sale
   d. where / wear

Zoom in p.42

Exercise 1:

HOMOGRAPHS: (possible answers)

English:

lives /lɪvz/ lives /laɪvz/	lead (v.) /li:d/ – (n.) /lɛd/
wind (n.) /wɪnd/ – (v.) /waɪnd/ tear (v.) /tɛr/ – (n.) – /tɪr/	Polish /ˈpoʊlɪʃ/ – polish /pɑlɪʃ/ close (v.) /kloʊz/ (adj) /kloʊs/

Portuguese:

colher (pick up) *colher (spoon)*	torre soco
bolo some	torno topo

HOMOPHONES (possible answers)

English:

stair stare	flower flour
meat meet	wear where

Portuguese:

concerto – conserto coser – cozer	russo – ruço tacha – taxa
sessão – seção passo – paço	acento – assento sela – cela

Why do you think that happens? It's harder to find examples in Portuguese because it is a phonetic language.

/fə'nætɪk fər fə'nɛtiks/ p.43

/si:/: *see / sea*	/meɪl/: mail / male
/'flaʊər/: flower / flour	/fɛr/: fare / fair
/roʊd/: rode / road	/meɪd/: maid / made
/wʊd/: wood / would	/noʊ/: no / know
/bɔrd/: bored / board	/ðɛr/: there / their / they're
/'haɪər/: hire / higher	/mi:t/: meet / meat
/pæst/: past / passed	/saɪt/: site / sight / cite
/'wɛðər/: weather / whether	/wɛr/: where / wear
/bɛr/: bare / bear	/baɪ/: bye / buy / by
/weɪ/: way / weigh	/pi:s/: piece / peace
/hi:l/: heel / heal	/daɪ/: die / dye
/breɪk/: brake / break	/kru:z/: cruise / crews
/sɛl/: sell / cell	/hu:z/: whose / who's

Fun time p.43

BIG SAIL HEAR AT MEYER'S & SUN

Big sale here at Meyer's & Son

SHOES: BY SUM NICE PEARS FOUR JUST ATE DOLLARS

Shoes: buy some nice pairs for just eight dollars

CLOSE: THE HOLE STOCK ON SAIL WITH SPECIAL PRICES. SEA THE VARIETY OF COLORS WE OFFER: YELLOW, READ, PINK AND BLEW

Clothes: the whole stock on sale with special prices. See the variety of colors we offer: yellow, red, pink and blue

DON'T WEIGHT! TOO WEAKS ONLY! BEE OUR SPECIAL GUESSED.

Don't wait! Two weeks only! Be our special guest.

OPENING OURS: FROM ATE TWO FOR (ON SATURDAY WE CLOTHES AT WON.)

Opening hours: from eight to four (On Saturday we close at one.)

KNEW ADDRESS: 36 KING RODE

New address: 36 King Road

Part B

Intro

Think about it p.47

1. egressive
2. lungs, trachea, larynx, mouth, nose
3. completely open

1. T
2. F
3. F

Zoom in p.48

/f/	VL	/ʃ/	VL
/v/	VD	/ʒ/	VD

Zoom in p.50

1. lips
2. teeth / lip
3. teeth
4. tongue
5. tongue
6. palate
7. air / folds

Unit 1

Think about it p.51

1. /ð/
2. /θ/
3. /ð/
4. /ð/
5. /θ/
6. /θ/

Zoom in p.52

Exercise 2:
1. Thursday; **2.** thin; **3.** math; **4.** teeth; **5.** north; **6.** thirty; **7.** athlete; **8.** thought; **9.** mouth; **10.** author

Stay tuned p.55

1. Is your sister three? (**a**)
2. Paul is sinking. (**b**)
3. Sheila has a beautiful mouth. (**b**)
4. Put the telephone in the booth. (**a**)
5. Bill and Gina fought for a while. (**b**)
6. Julia loves math. (**a**)

Stay tuned p.58

1. dare /d/; **2.** they /ð/; **3.** dough /d/; **4.** then /ð/; **5.** there /ð/; **6.** doze /d/; **7.** day /d/; **8.** though /ð/; **9.** den /d/; **10.** those /ð/

/fəˈnætɪk fər fəˈnɛtɪks/ p.59

a.6; **b.**4; **c.**10; **d.**3; **e.**9; **f.**5; **g.**8; **h.**1; **i.**7; **j.**2

Fun time p.60

(some possible answers)

an ordinal number: third, tenth
a quality:trustworthy, truthful
a demonstrative pronoun: this, that
a part of the house: bathroom
a material: leather
a noise from nature: thunder

a preposition: through
a family member: brother, father
a name: Ruth, Faith (***not*** Thomas)
a part of the body: mouth, thigh
a profession: author, athlete
a public building: theater

Unit 2

Get your tongue around it p.63

the team – coming – good – rhyme

Conversation p.64

Jim: Tom, we have a problem: we have to bom~~b~~ the colum~~n~~ or we won't be able to get into the tom~~b~~.
Tom: Jim! We have to com~~b~~ the field before we bom~~b~~ it, or the walls will go to crum~~b~~s and we might destroy something important.
Jim: OK, Tom.

Get your tongue around it p.66

Exercise 2:

employees – insects – offices – umbrellas

/fə'nætɪk fər fə'nɛtɪks/ p.71

1 d. The angel was combing seven lambs on the mountain.
2 b. One cute lamb dreamed of an angel calmly singing in the rain.
3 a. The lamb climbed the mountain and found something strange.
4 c. A charming lamb was eating ice cream on the dangerous rim of the mountain.

Unit 3

/fə'nætɪk fər fə'nɛtɪks/ p.76

a.3; **b.**8; **c.**1; **d.**6; **e.**9 **f.**5; **g.**10; **h.**2; **i.**7; **j.**4

Stay tuned p.79

1. rat
2. Hide
3. you're right
4. rose
5. hound
6. habit
7. Rome
8. red
9. rare
10. hated

Unit 4

Get your tongue around it p.85

Exercise 2:

they – understand – she – observe – we – explain – I – eat

Stay tuned p.87

Exercise 3:

1. sold
2. bow
3. Go
4. colt
5. role
6. code

/fə'nætɪk fər fə'nɛtɪks/ p.88

1. f – school; **2.** e – jewel; **3.** g – child; **4.** h – loyal; **5.** d – small; **6.** c – needle; **7.** a – hospital; **8.** b – whole

Fun time p.89

"You can *fool all* the *people* some of the time, and some of the *people all* the time, but you cannot *fool all* the *people all* of the time."

Unit 5

Think about it p.91

1. **F** – Although the sounds are the same, the Portuguese /p/ is not aspirated.
2. **F** – /t/ is aspirated, /d/ is not.
3. **T** – They're aspirated.
4. **F** – /k/ is aspirated in initial and stressed position.

Conversation p.95

Kate: Hi, **T**e**d**. **T**om jus**t** **c**alled as**k**ing if you **c**oul**d** len**d** him your vi**d**eo **c**amera.

Ted: Than**k**s for **t**elling me, **K**a**te**. I**t**'s abou**t** **t**ime **T**om bough**t** his own e**quip**ment, **d**on'**t** you thin**k**? I**t**'s the **t**en**t**h time he's as**ked** **t**o borrow mine!

Kate: Be **p**atient, **T**e**d**. Af**t**er all, **T**om jus**t** wan**t**s **t**o shoo**t** his **c**ousin's birth**d**ay **p**ar**t**y.

Ted: O**K**. When's the o**cc**asion?

Kate: O**c**t**o**ber four**t**eenth.

Ted: So **T**om's **g**oing to **b**e the cinema**t**ographer a**t** *my* **g**e**t**-**t**o**g**ether? So wha**t** are we wai**t**ing for? **T**om nee**d**s tha**t** **c**am**c**order righ**t** away!

Stay tuned p.97

2. b – beet/beach; **3.** a – tin/chin; **4.** a – cat/catch; **5.** b – eat/each; **6.** a – two/chew; **7.** b – tip/chip

Stay tuned p.99

1. Dean; **2.** G; **3.** aid; **4.** jig; **5.** beach; **6.** cat

In context p.101

Exercise 2:

Jack and Bob are brothers. They would like a new car, so they got a job at a supermarket. Jack is a cashier at the check-out counter, and Bob is an attendant at Customer Service. One day, Jack found a bag of groceries under the counter. Jack opened it, and found a lot of money inside. Bob almost couldn't believe his eyes, and wanted to spend it all right away. Jack insisted that they return the bag to the police. Bob agreed and they did it. They were very happy to hear there was a reward. The reward allowed them to get their car and quit the job at the supermarket.

/fə'nætɪk fər fə'nɛtɪks/ p.102

The angry king proclaimed that the princess couldn't buy a pet porcupine.

Unit 6

Think about it p.103

1.g; **2.**d

Stay tuned p.105

Exercise 2:

1. Jack fell down and hurt his shin. (**a**)
2. This is a chocolate ship. (**b**)
3. Would you like to try this cherry? (**b**)
4. Mr. Bush just called. (**a**)
5. I don't like this chore. (**b**)

6. Will you watch the car for me? (**b**)
7. Cash that check! (**a**)
8. She has a wish. (**a**)

In context p.108

Mitch and Sean share a cheap shack by the shore. Mitch usually catches a coach to the beach to go fishing on weekends. Sean, on the other hand, much prefers to drive his Chevy down to the shore in March, when there aren't kids shouting all around, so he can sit on a bench and watch the sea in peace. Mitch and Sean never go to the shack together, and they think their arrangement is perfect!

Think about it p.109

1.F; **2.**F; **3.**T; **4.**T; **5.**T

Conversation p.111

Exercise 2:

1. /ʃ/ – Sheila, Sean, wished, special, sure, punishment, should, posh
2. /tʃ/ – picture, purchase, chance, search, natural, exchange, watch
3. /ʒ/ – usually, treasure, Parisian
4. /dʒ/ – *just*, courage, Gina, Japanese

Think about it p.113

1. (possible answers)

f: leaf, if, chief, wolf, loaf
ff: cliff, cuff, stuff, off
fe: wife, safe, life, knife

ph: elephant, pharmacy, autograph
gh: enough, cough, laugh, rough

2. **a.**/v/; **b.**/f/

3. d

4. T

/fə'nætɪk fər fə'nɛtɪks/ p.116

which /tʃ/	judge /dʒ/ /dʒ/	situation /tʃ/ /ʃ/
changing /tʃ/ /dʒ/	education /dʒ/ /ʃ/	physician /f/ /ʃ/
tough /f/	Indonesian /ʒ/	childish /tʃ/ /ʃ/

Unit 7

Think about it p.117

1. **F** – There's just one syllable.
2. **T**
3. **F** – *This* ends in /s/ and *these* ends in /z/.
4. **T**
5. **F** – /yɛsɪtɪz/.
6. **F** – The first is pronounced /z/ and the second is pronounced /s/.

Get your tongue around it p.120

Exercise 1:

class – smart – mouse – mouse – scary – sleepy – nurse
dishonest – niece – famous

Exercise 2:

Can you speak English?
Do you watch TV every day?
Will you help me?
Have you been practicing pronunciation?
Did you talk on the phone yesterday?

Zoom in p.122

Exercise 2:

a.2/3; **b.**1; **c.**2/3; **d.**2 **e.**1; **f.**3

Zoom in p.124

Exercise 3:

What's the **use** of buying it if you don't **use** it?
Close one of **these** windows and sit **close** to me.
Excuse us, but **this** isn't a good **excuse**.
You shouldn't **house** a pet in your **house**.
If you let it **loose**, you might **lose** it.

Stay tuned p.124

1. prize
2. face
3. raise
4. eyes
5. once

/fə'nætɪk fər fə'nɛtɪks/ p.125

A	E	R	T	H	I	O	L	L	S	T	R	A	I	G	H	T
K	I	J	N	L	O	O	S	E	V	C	F	T	H	O	U	H
S	E	Z	O	R	E	S	N	I	O	P	L	Z	S	V	B	O
E	N	D	I	V	O	L	P	A	I	S	O	N	S	Z	A	Q
Q	W	E	R	T	Y	D	I	O	P	P	A	S	C	D	F	G
K	L	Z	X	C	V	E	N	M	M	E	T	E	I	R	N	I
C	R	O	S	D	E	S	S	E	R	T	A	I	S	N	O	S
E	C	R	A	F	M	E	O	T	B	O	N	G	S	T	I	N
S	Q	U	E	G	L	R	I	Z	I	B	A	S	O	A	I	L
U	T	E	A	H	C	T	E	R	S	T	U	D	R	E	N	T
B	K	L	O	I	N	G	E	V	I	G	R	X	S	T	Y	N
T	D	A	I	D	E	T	P	P	H	A	N	M	D	S	I	M
U	N	I	V	N	R	T	Y	C	R	O	L	A	S	A	Y	S
O	E	E	T	A	U	I	O	P	L	I	L	K	J	H	G	F
A	S	F	C	L	A	Q	X	S	W	T	S	R	F	V	B	N
B	R	A	N	S	N	H	A	P	E	D	R	M	O	M	Y	L
Q	A	Z	X	I	W	E	E	D	C	V	S	R	I	E	H	T
D	U	E	R	G	H	T	E	R	L	U	A	G	H	B	Y	C
S	K	E	I	T	B	O	R	D	G	E	N	E	R	O	U	S

Unit 8

Think about it p.127

Exercise 1:

1.F; **2.**F; **3.**T; **4.**T

Exercise 2:

Europe cure million	uniform year university	quite equal liquid	language one persuade

/y/ and /w/ are semi-vowels, so your tongue glides (moves) for the production of these sounds, and /i:/ and /u:/ are vowels.

Get your tongue around it p.130

Exercise 2:

1. ears
2. year
3. ears
4. ear
5. years
6. years
7. ears
8. year

The silent corner p.132

Exercise 2:

wrap – rap
write – right
whole – hole

/fəˈnætɪk fər fəˈnɛtɪks/ p.133

Once you persuade European women to wear something, the rest of the world will follow.

Fun time p.133

Exercise 1:

a.7; **b.**5; **c.**2; **d.**4; **e.**3; **f.**6; **g.**1

Exercise 2:

1. We are born naked, wet and hungry. Then things get worse.
2. Where there's a will, I want to be in it.
3. Always remember you're unique, just like everyone else.
4. When everything's coming your way, you're in the wrong lane.
5. By the time we realize our parents were right, we have children who think we're wrong.
6. We have enough youth, how about a fountain of smart?
7. When you don't know what you are doing, do it neatly.

Unit 9

Think about it p.135

1. In the plural, possessives, third person singular and contractions.
2. No. It can be pronounced /s/, /z/ or /ɪz/.
3. cats – /s/; apples – /z/, watches – /ɪz/.

Get your tongue around it p.140

1. James's umbrella
2. Charles's arm
3. Chris's eraser
4. Alice's orange
5. the judge's armchair
6. the fox's eye

Stay tuned p.141

Exercise 1:

1. passes /ɪz/ – **2.** pencils /z/ – **3.** parks /s/ – **4.** shirts/s/ – **5.** watches /ɪz/
6. cars /z/ – **7.** cups /s/ – **8.** bananas /z/ – **9.** bridges /ɪz/ – **10.** homes /z/

Exercise 2:

	add a sound	add a syllable
passes		x
hopes	x	
kisses		x
snake's	x	
goes	x	
massages		x
Kate's	x	
catches		x
caves	x	
judge's		x
noses		x
studies	x	

In context p.142

Bill wakes up at seven, that is, his alarm clock goes off at seven, but he never gets up right away. He enjoys staying in bed for five or ten minutes longer. He rarely takes a shower in the morning, as he is usually late. He only washes his face, brushes his teeth and shaves. Then he changes clothes, drinks a cup of coffee and eats some bread. He leaves for work at seven-forty. Work begins at eight.

/s/	/z/	/ɪz/
wakes	goes	washes
gets	enjoys	brushes
takes	shaves	changes
drinks	leaves	
eats	begins	

/fəˈnætɪk fər fəˈnɛtɪks/ p.143

passes	/ˈpæsɪz/	massages	/məˈsɑʒɪz/
hopes	/hoʊps/	Kate's	/keɪts/
studies	/ˈstʌdiz/	catches	/ˈkætʃɪz/
kisses	/ˈkɪsɪz/	caves	/keɪvz/
snake's	/sneɪks/	judge's	/ˈdʒʌdʒɪz/
goes	/goʊz/	noses	/ˈnoʊzɪz/

Fun time p.143

/s/	/z/	/ɪz/
carrots	strawberries	peaches
nuts	melons	oranges
coconuts	bananas	radishes
grapes	cucumbers	
beets (beetroots)	mushrooms	

Unit 10

Think about it p.145

Exercise 1:

/t/, /d/, /ɪd/

Exercise 2:

1. a. (1)
   b. (1)
2. a. (2)
   b. (2)
3. a. (1)
   b. (2)
4. a. (1)
   b. (1)
5. a. (1)
   b. (2)
6. a. (1)
   b. (1)

Get your tongue around it p.148

Exercise 2:

a.6; **b.**8; **c.**9; **d.**1; **e.**3; **f.**2; **g.**4; **h.**7; **i.**5

Zoom in p.149

Exercise 2:

aloud
band
build
find
side
tide

In context p.150

Exercise 1:

1 syllable	2 syllables	3 syllables
warned	prepared	disobeyed
strolled	preferred	
loved	opened	
lived	hurried	
feared	devoured	
hummed	arrived	
	worried	

Exercise 2:

1. hummed; **2.** strolled; **3.** loved; **4.** preferred; **5.** warned; **6.** lived; **7.** worried; **8.** disobeyed; **9.** fear**ed**; **10.** hurri**ed**; **11.** arriv**ed**; **12.** open**ed**; **13.** devour**ed**; **14.** prepar**ed**

Zoom in p.151

Exercise 1:

1. (2)	3. (2)	5. (1)	7. (4)
2. (3)	4. (3)	6. (2)	8. (5)

Stay tuned p.153

1.c; **2.**a; **3.**b; **4.**b; **5.**a; **6.**b; **7.**c; **8.**a

/fə'nætık fər fə'nɛtıks/ p.155

plan	/plæn/	relax	/rı'læks/	need	/ni:d/
	/plænd/		/rı'lækst/		/'ni:dıd/
wash	/wɑʃ/	arrive	/ə'raıv/	hate	/heıt/
	/wɑʃt/		/ə'raıvd/		/'heıtıd/
thank	/θæŋk/	record	/rı'kɔrd/	measure	/'mɛʒər/
	/θæŋkt/		/rı'kɔrdıd/		/'mɛʒərd/
climbed	/klaım/	protest	/prə'tɛst/	breathe	/bri:ð/
	/klaımd/		/prə'tɛstıd/		/bri:ðd

Part C

Intro

Zoom in p.163

kítchen	compúter	confúsion	fámous
stómach	éxcellent	nécklace	prívate

Zoom in p.165

hypothesis	/haɪˈpɑθəsɪs/
technology	/tɛkˈnɑlədʒɪ/
justify	/ˈjʌstəfaɪ/
operator	/ˈɑpəˌreɪtər/
female	/ˈfiːˌmeɪl/
organize	/ˈɔrgənaɪz/
television	/ˈtɛləˌvɪʒən/
guarantee	/ˌgɛrənˈti/
teenager	/ˈtiːnˌeɪdʒər/
acrobat	/ˈækrəˌbæt/

Unit 1

Think about it p.167

1. No. Heat /hi:t/ and hit /hɪt/.
2. c
3. a. /i:/
   b. possible answers: ee (meet) – ea (sea) – e (be) – ey (key) – ei (receive) – ie (believe) i (ski)

Zoom in p.169

Exercise 2:

ee or ea

Zoom in p.171

Exercise 2:

The sound /ɪ/ is usually spelled with the letter i between consonants or in initial position followed by a consonant.

Zoom in p.173

Exercise 2:

Cindy and Rita are busy women, but they manage to keep fit.
Will Peter sit and listen?
Athletes wish the system weren't tricky.
Please dear, be clear.

Stay tuned p.173

Exercise 1 & 2:

1. Was Tom bitten? (**b**)
2. Martha bought a big sheep. (**a**)
3. Harry had a huge feast. (**a**)
4. Is he going to live? (**b**)
5. That was an awful scene. (**a**)
6. If you don't pay attention, you might slip. (**b**)
7. I can't fill the pan. (**b**)

Exercise 3:

1. beaten; **2.** ship; **3.** fist; **4.** leave; **5.** sin; **6.** sleep; **7.** feel

Fun time p.175

(possible answers)

/i:/		/ɪ/	
feet	teeth	fist	wrist
cheek	knee	shin	lip
heel	spleen	finger	chin
		ear	beard
		hip	liver

/fəˈnætɪk fər fəˈnɛtɪks/ p.176

1. /ɪr/; **2.** /lɪp/; **3.** /ti:θ/; **4.** /tʃi:k/; **5.** /tʃɪn/; **6.** /rɪst/; **7.** /ˈfɪŋgər/; **8.** /hɪp/; **9.** /ni:/; **10.** /ʃɪn/; **11.** /fi:t/; **12.** /hi:l/

Unit 2

Think about it p.177

1. No, man /mæn/ and men /mɛn/.
2. Yes, because we don't have these sounds in Portuguese and they are very similar to our ***é***.
3. Interconsonantal *a* and *a* in stressed initial position followed by a consonant.
4. a. /ɛ/; b. é; c. /æ/

Zoom in p.179

Exercise 2:

The sound /ɛ/ can be spelled with the letter e between consonants, or in initial position followed by a consonant.

Zoom in p.181

Exercise 2:

/æ/ is usually spelled with the letter a between consonants, or in initial position followed by a consonant.

Exercise 4:

/ɪ/	/æ/
sing	sang
swim	swam
drink	drank
begin	began
sit	sat
shrink	shrank

Exercise 5:

M**a**tt s**a**t down, dr**a**nk bl**a**ck rum and s**a**ng s**a**dly.
S**a**m sw**a**m till his p**a**nts shr**a**nk.
P**a**m beg**a**n to ch**a**t with N**a**t in J**a**nuary.

Stay tuned p.183

1. vat; **2.** pan; **3.** Brad; **4.** celery; **5.** bat; **6.** sad; **7.** sexes; **8.** men

/fə'nætɪk fər fə'nɛtiks/ p.185

1./æ/; **2.**/ɛ/; **3.**/æ/; **4.**/æ/; **5.**/ɛ/; **6.**/ɛ/; **7.**/ɛ/; **8.**/æ/; **9.**/æ/; **10.**/æ/–/æ/; **11.**/ɛ/; **12.**/ɛ/–/ɛ/

Fun time p.186

(possible answers)

month	/ɛ/: February /æ/: January	country	/ɛ/: Belgium /æ/: France
animal	/ɛ/: elephant /æ/: cat	part of the house	/ɛ/: bedroom /æ/: bathroom
food	/ɛ/: pear, lemon /æ/: apple, banana	color	/ɛ/: red, yellow /æ/: black
object	/ɛ/: pen /æ/: pan	place around town	/ɛ/: hotel /æ/: bank

Unit 3

Think about it p.187

1. The words in the question contain the /ʊ/ sound and the words in the answer contain the /u:/ sound.
2. /u:/
3. /ʊ/
4. /u:/
5. /u:/

Zoom in p.189

Exercise 5:

1. room
2. new
3. future
4. brooms

5. few
6. two
7. boots
8. blue
9. pool
10. truth

Get your tongue around it p.190

1. He said he shook the butcher's hand.
2. He said he put on a hood to avoid the soot.
3. He said he stood up to greet Brooke.
4. He said he could go to the brook on foot.
5. He said he would push the poor wolf.
6. He said he looked good.
7. He said he understood the cookbook.

Stay tuned p.192

2./u:/; **3.**/ʊ/; **4.**/u:/; **5.**/ʊ/; **6.**/ʊ/; **7.**/u:/; **8.**/ʊ/; **9.**/u:/; **10.**/u:/, **11.**/ʊ/, **12.**/ʊ/

/fəˈnætɪk fər fəˈnɛtɪks/ p.194

a.2; **b.**3; **c.**4; **d.**6

Unit 4

Think about it p.195

1.

a.T; **b.**F; **c.**F; **d.**T

2.

/ɑ/ as in *bar*	/ɔ/ as in *four*
s**er**geant	t**a**lk
h**ea**rt	c**a**ll
br**a**	l**aw**
g**ua**rd	w**a**r
c**a**lm	**au**thor

Stay tuned p.200

Polly and Mark wanted to buy presents for their family, so they went to the shopping mall. Polly got a bottle of scotch for her father, but Mark just got socks. Polly got some body lotion for their mother, but Mark only got a cheap clock. Polly got a Barbie doll for their little sister, but Mark only got a box of chocolates. Polly got a toy rocket for their little brother, but Mark only got him a pet rock. Polly shouted at Mark, "Stop! I'm shocked! What are you going to get me, then? A washcloth?" Mark replied, "Right on the dot!"

In context p.200

1.f; **2.**e; **3.**d; **4.**c; **5.**g; **6.**a; **7.**b

/fəˈnætɪk fər fəˈnɛtɪks/ p.201

It was *prom* night, and all the seniors at St. George High School were very excited. There was going to be a rock band, and they promised to play all the most popular songs. Some of the girls spent thousands of dollars on her dresses, and boys bought them the most beautiful corsages at the mall. All the boys wore white collars and ties and music could be heard all around the block. It was a night they would recall for the rest of their lives.

Unit 5

Think about it p.203

1. No, but sometimes they mispronounce words with these sounds, producing other vowel sounds due to spelling.

2. /ʌ/ is stressed and /ə/ is unstressed.

3. The vowel sound in these words is /ʌ/.

4.

/ʌ/	/ɜr/	/ə/ /ʌ/	/ə/ /ɜr/	/ɜr/ /ə/	/ʌ/
much	search	above	occur	curtain	son

Conversation p.207

/ʌ/	/ɜr/	/ɜrl/
mother	purchase	pearl (s)
young	birthday	world
love	turn	curls
done	thirty	girlfriend
one		Earl
		girl (s)

Stay tuned p.208

1. a, **2.** b, **3.** b, **4.** a; **5.** a

Zoom in p.209

Exercise 2:

It's h**o**t in this c**ou**ntry.
L**o**ck the h**u**t or tr**u**st your l**u**ck.
My p**u**ppy ate all the p**o**ppies in the g**a**rden.
My h**ea**rt h**u**rts.
There's **o**ne b**u**ck in the b**o**x.
I h**ea**rd about the h**a**rd w**or**k.
Don't b**o**ther my br**o**ther, my f**a**ther or my m**o**ther.

Stay tuned p.210

1. There was a bomb on the street. (**a**)
2. Did you leave the cup in the kitchen? (**b**)
3. This is my buddy. (**b**)
4. That's a big knot. (**a**)
5. There's a duck in my backyard. (**b**)
6. "Fond of money" is hard to define. (**b**)
7. What color do you prefer? (**b**)

/fə'nætɪk fər fə'nɛtiks/ p.211

/fæn/	*fan*	/hɑt/	hot
/fɪn/	*fin*	/hæt/	hat
/fʌn/	*fun*	/hʌt/	hut
		/hɜrt/	hurt
/lɑk/	lock	/hɑrt/	heart
/lʊk/	look		
/læk/	lack	/bɑks/	box
/lʌk/	luck	/bʊks/	books
/li:k/	leak / leek	/bʌks/	bucks
/fɜrm/	firm	/bɜrd/	bird
/fɑrm/	farm	/bɔrd/	bored / board
/fɔrm/	form	/bɪrd/	beard

Unit 6

Think about it p.215

1. Because /o/ and /e/ don't exist as pure vowels in English, speakers tend to follow the patterns of their own language.

2. Yes, as the preceding vowel is pronounced as its alphabetical value.

3.

/eɪ/	/oʊ/
danger	though
bracelet	bowl
steak	sole
valet	toe
main	sew
freight	Joan
obey	obey

Zoom in p.217

Exercise 2:

a. ai or ay
b. C a C + silent e

Stay tuned p.222

Exercise 3:

1. men
2. cold
3. claim
4. toll
5. trend
6. bow
7. sole / soul
8. main
9. trained
10. bowl

In context p.223

Exercise 2:

1.d; **2.**f; **3.**h; **4.**c; **5.**g; **6.**b; **7.**e; **8.**a

/fəˈnætɪk fər fəˈnɛtɪks/ p.224

/ʌ/	/ɜr/	/ɑ/	/ɔ/
buck	third	sock	saw
truck	bird	lock	straw
/ɛ/	/æ/	/iː/	/ɪ/
net	cat	feet	kill
pet	hat	eat	hill
/eɪ/	/oʊ/	/uː/	/ʊ/
train	*note*	flute	book
plane	*boat*	boot	cook

Fun time p.225

Set 1

1. a, d, g
2. c, f, h
3. b, e, i

Set 2

1. b, f, h
2. a, d, g
3. c, e, i

Unit 7

Think about it p.227

1. **a.**3; **b.**2; **c.**1; **d.**1; **e.**3; **f.**1; **g.**2; **h.**1

2. Possible answers: boy, about, pie, kite, oil, night, clown, my

3. Read Close Up to check your answer.

Zoom in p.231

Exercise 2:

1.g; **2.**e; **3.**a; **4.**b; **5.**h; **6.**c; **7.**d; **8.**f

Exercise 3:

1./ɪ/; **2.**/ɪ/; **3.**/aɪ/; **4.**/aɪ/; **5.**/ɪ/; **6.**/u:/; **7.**/aʊ/; **8.**/ɪ/; **9.**/aɪ/; **10.**/aʊ/; **11.**/oʊ/

Get your tongue around it p.232

Exercise 1:

human – modern – formal – legal – sympathy – central – energy

Exercise 2:

simple – note – beauty – class – glory – false

Exercise 3:

satisfaction – certification – qualification – modification – magnification – justification

Stay tuned p.233

Exercise 1:

1. dyed; **2.** dinner; **3.** filed; **4.** stripes; **5.** prim; **6.** kit; **7.** rhyme

Fun time p.234

a. 2 – brown; **b.** 3 – boy; **c.** 1 – buy; **d.** 3 – toys; **e.** 1 – mine; **f.** 2 – town;

g. 3 – voice; **h.** 1 – side; **i.** 3 – noise; **j.** 2 – crowd; **k.** 1 – right; **l.** 1 – night; **m.** 1 – 1 – five – nine; **n.** 2 – shout; **o.** 2 – now; **p.** 3 – choice; **q.** 3 – boil; **r.** 2 – mouse; **s.** 2 – couch

/fəˈnætɪk fər fəˈnɛtɪks/ p.236

		1 æ	k	s		2 k	3 æ	4 tʃ		
5 b	i:	t			6 k	ʌ	m	ɪ	ŋ	
æ					7 ɔ	t		n		
8 θ	9 ɔ	t	10 f	ʊ	l		11 b			
	r		ɪ			12 t	ɛ	r		13 ʃ
	14 b	15 ɪ	l	16 b	ɔ	r	d		17 ð	oʊ
18 b	ɪ	r		ʊ		ʌ			æ	
	t			19 tʃ	ɑ	k	l	20 ə	t	
				ə				d		
	21 aɪ	s	22 k	r	i:	m		22 r	eɪ	22 s
25 ɪ	l		26 i:	z				ɛ		ɔɪ
	27 z	u:	z		28 tʃ	æ	n	s		

How to listen to the audio

Todo o conteúdo em áudio referente a este livro, você poderá encontrar em qualquer uma das seguintes plataformas:

DEEZER

Ao acessar qualquer uma dessas plataformas, será necessário a criação de uma conta de acesso (poderá ser a versão gratuita). Após, pesquise pelo título completo do livro, ou pelo autor ou ainda por **Disal Editora**, localize o álbum ou a playlist e você terá todas as faixas de áudio mencionadas no livro.

Para qualquer dúvida, entre em contato com **marketing@disaleditora.com.br**

IMPORTANTE:
Caso você venha a encontrar ao longo do livro citações ou referências a CDs, entenda como o áudio acima indicado.

Este livro foi composto em Bliss, SIL Doulos IPA e
Times New Roman PS e impresso em setembro de 2024
pela Paym Gráfica e Editora Ltda., sobre papel offset 75g/m^2.